Shaping the Future

Shaping the Future

Foreign Policy in an Age of Transition

by Robert R. Bowie

Columbia University Press
New York and London, 1964

Robert R. Bowie is Director of the Center for International Affairs and Dillon Professor of International Affairs at Harvard University. This book was written at the Center for International Affairs.

Foreword

The William Radner lectures were established at Columbia University in 1956 as a memorial to Mr. Radner, a graduate of Columbia College and the Columbia Law School, whose untimely death cut short a brilliant and promising career devoted to the public service of his country. In creating this most fitting memorial, Mr. Radner's family made no stipulation other than that the lectures should be devoted to the public policies and the public service of the United States.

The first Radner lectures were given in the spring of 1959 by former President Harry S. Truman. Subsequently published, these lectures created wide interest because of the wealth of personal experience from which the President could draw for his observations upon the constitutional and political role of the Presidency.

For the second series, it seemed appropriate to consider the great and complex field of foreign policy and administration which occupies an ever-increasing importance in the totality of our government's operations. The faculty selection committee was understandably gratified when Professor Robert Bowie, former Assistant Secretary of State and currently the Director of the Center for International Affairs at Harvard, accepted its invitation to become the 1963 Radner Lecturer. His analysis of the requisites for successful foreign policy-planning, the difficulties of fusing planning with action, and his case study of the search for order in the Atlantic Community, combine to supply the thoughtful reader with many new and useful insights. Like that of his predecessor, Professor Bowie's book will find a wide audience— and deservedly so.

GRAYSON KIRK

Columbia University
in the City of New York
January, 1964

Preface

This volume contains the Radner Lectures which I gave at Columbia University in April, 1963. For the privilege of doing so, and for the cordial hospitality during my visit, I am deeply indebted to the President and Faculty of the University, and especially to the members of the Faculty of Political Science.

The subject—foreign policy in an era of radical change—obviously could not be covered in three lectures. They should be viewed as essays approaching the topic from several directions. The first lecture attempts to distill from the postwar experience key features for foreign policy designed to influence an emerging world order. In the second, the demands of such policy are analyzed with reference to European and Atlantic relations as a specific case study. Finally, the third lecture examines how the United States government can organize and manage its diverse activities to meet the requisites for effective long-term policy.

In preparing the lectures for publication, I have revised a few passages in the interest of clarity, without changing the substance. It is a pleasure to express my thanks to my colleague, Thomas Schelling, for comments during the writing and to Max Hall for generous editorial assistance.

ROBERT R. BOWIE

Cambridge, Massachusetts
November, 1963

Contents

I

The Requisites for
Policy Today

Our epoch faces the unprecedented task of organizing and defending a new global order congenial to freedom. The upheavals of five decades have swept away the world order inherited from the last century. The present era is a stage of transition between the outmoded past and an emerging order still largely obscured by mists.

The fashioning of that new international system will doubtless extend over many decades. Its creation will not be sudden or dramatic; nor can it be put off or postponed. Within limits and imperatives imposed by the basic forces of our time, it will be molded gradually by day-to-day actions, taken routinely or in crisis, by our own and other nations.

The influence of even a powerful state on this future order will depend largely on the cumulative impact of its manifold actions over time, and on how far they reinforce one another and are concerted with those of others. To attain such coherence, decisions and activities must be organized and managed for the steady pursuit of sound long-term purposes. To do this in a turbulent world of conflict and change is a formidable challenge. How to do it seems to me the crucial problem for a foreign policy adequate to our time. That is the theme of this book.

The main features of a viable order compatible with freedom can be readily identified in general terms. First, it must build on and serve the deep mutual dependence among nations and regions, which constantly grows more intimate. Today no part of the globe is really remote from any other; actions anywhere may have their impact at the opposite pole. The nuclear threat only dramatizes this wider reality. External forces impinge more and more on domestic affairs making the line between them less and less distinct. National security and welfare cannot be found alone. Second, a new order will have to overcome strong divergent forces: the dedication of the Soviet Union and China, though feuding, to extending conformity in the Communist image; the tensions and distrust arising from the poverty, instability, and sensitive nationalism of the less-developed countries; and the cleavages among the Atlantic nations resulting from disparities in power and outlook. Third, the new order will have to preserve as much room as is feasible for diversity of societies and cultures.

The necessity to construct such an international order in an age of revolution—political, social, industrial, and scientific—is an immense undertaking. The scope and complexity of the challenge have not been quickly realized. The history of international affairs since World War II can be thought of as the gradual discovery of the basic forces shaping our era, and the devising of actions and policies to respond to them or to try to control or modify them. Governments and their citizens did not identify these realities all at once, but learned their nature gradually through experience.

One way to clarify the nature of the tasks facing us and the requisites for policies adequate to cope with them is to examine some of the experience in making and executing foreign policy since World War II. In considering three segments, my aim will be to identify and dissect the main components of effective policy oriented toward future order under modern conditions.

CONTAINMENT

The policy of containment offers a good starting point for this analysis. Its origin and history aptly show that the foundation for an effective policy must be a correct appraisal of the situation and consensus on a suitable strategy for coping with it.

In the postwar period, both elements were lacking at the start. The planning for the postwar world had been based on the premise that the victors would work together for their security and welfare in the United Nations and other international agencies, in occupying the defeated countries, and in the postwar settlements. Since that premise proved to be misconceived, the policies springing from it were stillborn.

Several years were required for the revision of this premise. As early as April, 1945, when Truman became President, Britain and the United States were already protesting the Soviet failure to live up to earlier agreements regarding Poland. Officials like Ambassador Harriman in Moscow and Secretary Forrestal in Washington argued then that the Soviet Union would follow its own expansionist policy. By February, 1946, George Kennan had sent in from Moscow his dispatch on the basis of Soviet policy which was later to appear in *Foreign Affairs* under the signature "X." And in March, 1946, Churchill made his speech at Fulton, Missouri, calling for joint action to oppose Soviet expansion.

But it was the impact of events—in Iran, Eastern Europe, Germany, Greece, and Turkey—which gradually convinced the Atlantic nations of Soviet hostility and of its dedication to expanding the area of Soviet control. Even so, not until the Greek-Turkish crisis in March, 1947, did the United States explicitly reorient its policy. Thereafter the events in Czechoslovakia, the Berlin blockade, and the Korean invasion substantiated this appraisal of the Communist threat.

Once the situation was reappraised, the doctrine of

containment matured into an agreed strategy as the foundation for practical joint measures. The concept was that Communism would "mellow" only if its expansion was frustrated over an extended period. Then the Communist regimes might reexamine the feasibility of their aims, revise their estimate of alternatives open to them, and modify their expansionist purposes or assign them much lower priority.

In achieving a consensus on this broad strategy, the Atlantic nations were greatly helped by the lessons of the 1930s. The experience with Hitler had taught that an aggressive, ideological power could not be stopped by compromise or by piecemeal actions. Most people were convinced that the threatened must stand together and must oppose expansion wherever it was attempted. This history made it far easier for President Truman and European leaders to mobilize support for collective defense of the Atlantic area, and for a strong stand against Communist expansion once the issues were clearly defined.

In his *Memoirs*, Mr. Truman has described how this set of ideas simplified for him the problem of Greece and Turkey in 1947. He recalls thinking at that time: "We had fought a long and costly war to crush the totalitarianism of Hitler, the insolence of Mussolini, and the arrogance of the war lords of Japan. Yet the new menace facing us seemed every bit as grave as Nazi Germany and her allies had been." [1] And in June, 1950, the attack on South Korea again revived these memories and their teachings.

Thus the parallel to the 1930s led to clear consensus. In the light of two world wars, the United States quickly perceived the bonds of interests which tied it to the fate of Europe. The stagnation of Europe and the threat of Communist takeover, especially in France and Italy, demanded a rapid and large-scale effort to assist in its economic recovery. But the threat was seen primarily as military aggression and the remedy as collective defense. It was essential for the United States to draw the line against further expansion in Europe; to join with European nations for collective defense in NATO; and to stand firm with any nation anywhere in the world threatened by Communist takeover.

The practical programs for collective defense have created controversy. In 1949, the NATO Treaty was a bipartisan measure in the United States and was widely supported in the weakened nations of Europe. NATO strategy and force goals, however, have been a continual source of friction and dispute. It is sufficient merely to recall the issues: the debate on U.S. forces for Europe, the rearming of Germany, the European Defense Community, the Lisbon force goals, the reliance on nuclear

---

[1] Harry S. Truman, *Memoirs* (New York, Doubleday, 1956), II, 101.

weapons, and the role of conventional forces. The reasons are not far to seek: these issues imposed financial or other burdens, which the Allies had to allot among themselves. Their solution also raised questions of military technology and weaponry on which knowledge was limited and debate extensive, even in the United States. And many of these involved conflicts with special interests or other programs of the various Allies.

Yet, despite these divergences, the principle of collective defense was applied with courage and continuity not only in Europe but in Asia and the Middle East. And the policy did largely deter or defeat aggression. By 1951, Communist control had been consolidated in Eastern Europe and had expanded into Czechoslovakia and mainland China. But in Iran, Greece, Turkey, Berlin, Korea, and the Formosa Straits, the Communists were blocked or thrown back by the Western response.

By closing the direct military route to expansion, the success of collective security forced the Communist regimes to review their policy in the light of changes since 1945. The outcome was the policy of "coexistence," developed between 1953 and 1956. It assumed that large-scale nuclear war was not a rational means for expansion; that a revived West Europe offered little prospect for early Communist advances; that the poor, unstable, less-developed areas were most suitable targets for infiltration and subversion; and that Soviet strength now allowed more varied techniques. "Coexistence" was a change in methods, not aims; a formula for vigorous struggle to expand by all means short of large-scale war. The hope was to divide the West by creating strains among the Atlantic allies and to make headway in the underdeveloped world by political, economic, propagandist, and subversive means.

The Soviets and Chinese Communists have not, however, eschewed the use of force. Indeed, they have been experimenting to determine how limited force and threats can still serve their policy. Laos and Vietnam are torn by guerrilla warfare and subversion. In Cuba, Soviet forces bolster the Castro regime despite its distance from Soviet borders. In India, the Chinese attacks have their political effects in South Asia. And Soviet pressure on Berlin has sought to use the fear of nuclear war as a lever for political gains.

The Sino-Soviet split arises in part from differing views on this strategy, and especially on how far force is still useful in pursuing Communist purposes. But according to their own testimony, both sides retain and pursue their dogmatic vision of a future Communist order. Their violent disputes, though serious, concern methods and tactics and primacy. The long-term effects cannot be predicted; but as things stand, the non-Communist nations still face the necessity of thwarting the efforts of either for a world of Communist conformity.

For the Atlantic nations, changed conditions have also required reappraisal and revision. The wider Communist challenge, which outruns the teachings of the 1930s, makes suitable basic purposes and policies even more essential and much harder to devise and pursue. Containment is still a valid objective, as far as it goes. The need to deter and oppose overt aggression remains; and indeed takes on enhanced importance as weapons become more deadly. But military capability is clearly only a partial answer to the challenge of coexistence. For an adequate reply, the West must undertake to build an international system compatible with its principles and values.

Indeed this constructive effort is essential for its own sake, as a response to growing interdependence. The Atlantic nations are linked—in varying degree—by a wide range of mutual interests in defense, economics, finance, monetary stability, and foreign affairs. The less-developed countries, in their turn, must look to the advanced nations for markets for their primary products and expanding manufactured exports, and for much technical and capital assistance. Indeed, even the Soviet Union has had to recognize a joint concern in avoiding a nuclear holocaust, while seeking to undermine the Western position by all other means.

In short, the task is now seen to have both a defensive and a constructive side. The defensive aspect is to prevent the Soviet Union and Communist China from imposing a world order which would have no place for societies like ours. The creative challenge is to develop a viable pluralist order which will serve the needs and aspirations of both the advanced and less-developed nations, with an empty chair for the Communist countries when they abandon their expansionism. The defensive and constructive aspects are, of course, inseparably linked: one cannot be accomplished without the other.

Our task is thus far more demanding than it appeared in the first postwar decade. True, that defensive phase required a more complete reversal of perspective and policies. But many factors made it simpler to identify common interests and concert on joint actions. The threat was more specific and clear cut, the lessons of the recent past more relevant, the appropriate response more obvious, and the leadership of the United States more taken for granted.

These simplifying factors are no longer present. The threat is more subtle and complex, and the affirmative effort to create a pluralist system is more difficult. The arena of policy has become more fluid: Soviet policy is more flexible, China pursues its own purposes and interests, a revived Europe is again a major factor, and some fifty new nations are on the world stage. The instruments of policy are more varied: politics and propaganda, aid and trade, exchanges of people and culture, and force, threats, and subversion—their impact is novel and uncertain.

In short, many more nations, differing widely in experience, outlook, and influence, must find ways of working together much more intimately. Under these conditions, the necessity of understanding the basic forces and of developing a strategic framework for long-term concerted action is far greater than in the late 1940s. The new complexities enhance both the need and the difficulties.

THE EUROPEAN COMMUNITY

The European Community represents a creative effort to build on the interdependence of its members. It is a striking example of what can be done with a bold conception, a practical program, and persistence.

The consensus on the Community was made possible by the experience of World War II and its aftermath. The idea of a United Europe has roots deep in the past, but it had never been able to overcome the nationalism and rivalries which divided Europe. On the Continent World War II shook the faith in the national state and in nationalism. The French were humiliated by their abrupt military collapse in 1940, and then by Nazi domination. Germany had endured the Nazi brutalities, utter defeat and chaos, and Allied occupation. Other nations on the Continent suffered similar ordeals.

With the memory of 1914 and earlier conflicts, these disasters and hardships eroded nationalist sentiments and prepared the way for practical steps toward European integration. In many countries, the Resistance produced some of the most ardent supporters for European unity. Their experience, drawing on loyalty to national ideals, often nurtured a vigorous sense of a common European destiny. With notable objectivity many of them came to see themselves, as well as their oppressors, as victims of the prior state system in Europe.

Even so, for five years action was hampered by the shackles of the past. Under British lead, the initial measures for European recovery and security were limited to familiar patterns of cooperation among sovereign states. Efforts to do more when creating the Organization for European Economic Cooperation and the Council of Europe met firm resistance from the United Kingdom. Another obstacle was the postwar policy toward defeated Germany. As after World War I, the Allies sought to control Germany and to keep her weak. Even when the Federal Republic of Germany was created in 1949, the Allies retained controls through the Allied High Commission, Military Control Board, and the International Authority for the Ruhr industries.

On the Continent, however, key statesmen made a more profound diagnosis of Europe's condition and needs. They concluded that Europe had outgrown its historic divisions and required radical treatment to assure its prosperity and security. They shared three dominant motives.

The first was to reconcile France and Germany. These men feared that the effort to keep Germany weak might reenact the prewar tragedy. They preferred her to become a full and equal partner in the creative task of building a united Europe. They hoped thereby to heal past wounds, forge firm links of common interest, and enlist the vital energies of the German people. So bold a reversal of existing policy toward Germany called for courage and leadership of the highest order.

The second motive was economic—to create a wider market in Europe. By 1950, the European economies had already started to revive under the impetus of the Marshall Plan. But could limited markets like France and Germany achieve the full advantages of technology and research? Many in Europe doubted it. The example of the United States suggested that a wider European market would foster a more dynamic economy with rising living standards and growing industries better able to compete in world trade.

The third motive was mainly political—to restore Europe's role in the world. With the revival of their economies and societies, Europeans naturally wanted a larger share in controlling their own fate. In industrial capacity, skilled people, and long tradition, Europe had the potential to play a major role in shaping a new world order. Yet the separate nations of Europe with their empires in liquidation were now overshadowed by two super-powers. For a greater role, some larger European entity would be needed to mobilize and use its resources.

In May, 1950, Robert Schuman, then French Foreign Minister, formulated the basic concept for European integration. On behalf of France, he officially proposed the long-term goal for a European Community leading ultimately to federation. This Community would be built on the premise that its members have common European interests which should transcend their separate interests. These wider interests should be expressed in common rules binding all members equally. And to administer and enforce these rules impartially, the Community required institutions based on a quasi-federal pattern. The response of Chancellor Adenauer and of the leaders in Italy and the Benelux countries was immediate and positive.

The vision of an ultimate federal or confederal entity —a United States of Europe—was surely an ambitious goal. To achieve it, if feasible at all, would be the work of several decades at best.

The crucial question was where and how to begin. What should be the intermediate objectives, the practical program? The Schuman proposal confronted this issue squarely. "A United Europe," it said, "will not be made all at once, or according to a single, general plan. It will be built by concrete achievements, which first create a solidarity in fact." Thus for a first step, Schuman suggested the creation of a Community for Coal and Steel—the sinews for past bloody struggle and for future prosperity. In entering such a Community, the Federal Republic had little to lose and much to gain. For France and the others, this was a bold and far-reaching action. In creating this first community they agreed to put their basic industry on the same footing as that of defeated Germany.

The concept of a European entity with common interests is at the heart of the European Community. In the original negotiations to create the Community in 1950–51, Jean Monnet for France and Walter Hallstein for the Federal Republic both approached the many complex issues in this spirit. Their method was to assure that "the parties all range themselves on one side of the table to confront the problem on the other side." The treaty which emerged reflected these principles in the institutions, the authority, and the rules for the Community.

The impartial Commission—the High Authority—is

charged with acting for the Community as an entity in identifying and promoting the common interests. Similarly, the Court of Justice is superior to the member states in applying the common rules. The European Parliament, though its powers are limited, is a symbol of the Community and serves as the voice of a unified Europe. Only the Council of Ministers, which has substantial authority under the Economic Community Treaty, represents the governments. But even the Council may increasingly decide by less than unanimity, which may enable the general interest to prevail over the parochial.

The progress in integration since the European Coal and Steel Community began to operate in 1952 is a tribute to the tenacity of its proponents and to the validity of their concept. As originally planned, the route has been marked by a series of partial steps. The pressure for rearming Germany in September, 1950, led to the effort to establish a European Defense Community and the companion Political Community. This proved premature and ended in failure in 1954. With that, many thought that integration would die. Yet hardly two years later, the six members of the Community had agreed to launch the far-reaching Economic Community and the Atomic Energy Community.

The Community has gained in vitality as it has achieved the purposes which inspired it. In its first decade, the Community has enabled Germany to rejoin the European family as a full member. The reconciling of France and Germany, which has contributed so much to the stability and strength of postwar Europe, is certainly one of the most dramatic benefits of integration.

In the economic field, also, the European Community has been a striking success. Even before the Common Market began, its members were enjoying rapid economic growth—much faster than that of the United States or the United Kingdom. Hence, its impact is hard to measure. Still, the Common Market has been an added stimulus to economic activity. The Community has materially speeded up the schedule fixed by the treaty for the removal of trade barriers. And business firms have been anticipating the wider market in making investments and locating plants.

The British decision in 1961 to apply for entry into the European Community was perhaps the most graphic testimony to its success. But General de Gaulle's abrupt rejection of Britain as a member at his press conference in January, 1963, has created a new situation, clouding the outlook for the Community. To that I will return in the next chapter.

Until de Gaulle's action, however, the movement for European integration had shown remarkable strength and persistence. The severe setback in 1954 after the defeat of EDC could have been its deathknell. But the conviction and courage of those Europeans who had fought for European unity were adequate to surmount even this handicap. With energy and imagination they revived the corpse and brought it back to a life far more vigorous than it had enjoyed before.

The Community is obviously still unfinished business. Conceivably, it could still founder. But the experience thus far provides valuable lessons in the process of knitting nations together by institutions and interests and by partial measures creating the basis for further advances. The progress of the Community testifies to the value of clear basic objectives and limited intermediate steps in organizing common efforts.

THE LESS-DEVELOPED COUNTRIES

The struggle to modernize in Asia, Africa, and Latin America will demand organized effort over decades. The primary effort must be indigenous, but steady outside support will be critical for capital, markets, technical help, and training. To provide effective support, the advanced West must work closely together and with the developing countries. A decade of experience has shown that such cooperation depends on consensus on long-term purposes and concerted programs of action. It has also revealed the serious obstacles to both requisites.

One barrier has been the gulf in outlook. That of the

less-developed countries, like our own, is colored by their history. Their colonial memory and present weakness inevitably make them extremely sensitive to real or imagined threats to their independence from any quarter, and predispose them to suspect the West of desires to reimpose its former control indirectly. At the same time, they have generally discounted the Western appraisal of Communist purposes. When the West was learning about Soviet expansionism from its menacing actions, the less-developed countries were almost wholly engrossed in their struggle for independence and growth. Hence, this part of history largely passed them by. Finally, the enormous disparity in economic, social, and political conditions inevitably creates a serious obstacle to understanding.

On its side, the West has also been confused in its approach to these developing nations. After Korea, our relations with those in Asia and the Middle East were often distorted by the drive for allies. Heavy assistance was provided to enable countries around the Communist periphery to maintain larger military forces for collective defense. In some areas, like Korea and Taiwan, stronger local forces may well have contributed to security and stability; but in others, alliances diverted to military purposes resources which might have been more valuable for economic growth. And the pressures for allies created friction with those, like India, who were not ready to commit themselves. Gradually the Western nations came to see more clearly that their primary interest was for the new nations to remain independent and at peace, and that alliances with them were not necessarily the most suitable way to provide for their security.

Thus help in modernizing their economies and societies has become the main focus of Western policy toward most of the less-developed countries. From the modest program for technical assistance launched by the Inaugural Address of President Truman in January, 1949, assistance to these nations has grown to an annual total of some $6 billion from the United States and other advanced nations.

Yet even while extending substantial aid, the West has often been uncertain about its purposes. Why should the advanced nations assist the less-developed to modernize? Various answers have been given; thus the recent Clay report enumerates the reasons for development assistance as follows: security, humanitarian concern, expanding export markets, assuring sources of necessary raw materials, and fostering global prosperity and peace.

These and other justifications have been criticized by various writers, such as Edward C. Banfield and Hans Morgenthau, on the grounds that the results of assistance are uncertain and difficult to relate to the interests of the assisting nation. My purpose here is not to evaluate either the justifications or the criticisms. It is to suggest that the lack of a consensus regarding the basic purposes makes it more difficult to conduct the programs on a long-term basis or to concert with other Western donors or to work with the recipient countries. And it makes it harder to resist the strong pull to use aid for more direct, short-run political benefits.

In seeking to devise and carry out agreed programs, the nature of the task is a further source of difficulties and frictions. The modernizing of a backward country is ultimately a political process. It requires the revamping of social and political structures and traditions as much as economic measures. The claims of consumption compete with those of saving and investment. Essential tax and land reforms will hurt those who now hold power. In many new states national cohesion is still too weak to overcome parochial loyalties. And political rivalries among leaders add to the instability and turmoil.

Each regime will strike its own balance among conflicting pressures and aims. Even where modernizing enjoys clear priority, the weakness of the government and lack of skilled officials or experts may severely hamper effective action. In consequence, many decisions will be ill advised; many projects will be badly executed; and there will be much waste and graft.

The leaders may also have other objectives and a different order of priorities than we may think appropriate, or than may be best suited for achieving rapid growth.

Some actions taken for political motives may interfere with the conditions for progress by their own country or by their neighbors. The Middle East and Indonesia offer excellent examples of such problems.

The Western nations, in carrying on their assistance programs, have an ambiguous relation with the governments of the recipient countries. Their transfers of capital and skills and other assistance are in part designed to induce the recipient government to use its own resources and to take other actions in the way best suited to modernizing its society. Hence assistance may be made dependent on fulfilling certain conditions of self-help and reform, as in the Alliance for Progress. This blend of cooperation and pressure creates a delicate relation. To avoid antagonism, the assisting nation must seek to convince the recipient that the required conditions are justified on balance.

There are severe limits to using assistance to influence domestic actions. Its tender or refusal may often be too weak a lever to induce a revision of purposes or priorities, especially where Communist aid offers a means to evade hard choices. The aiding nations face a baffling dilemma where privileged groups block essential reforms. Assistance may perpetuate their hold on power and delay needed actions; but withholding aid may risk instability and disorder, jeopardizing the security of the developing country.

Finally, the extended time required for positive results puts a premium on persistence and continuity, but also makes them hard to achieve. In most countries, the rate of progress in industry, agriculture, and education is almost sure to fall short of the hopes of the leaders and people. And even steady growth will benefit the ordinary citizen only slowly, especially while population increases so fast. Faltering progress can readily breed frustration, demagoguery, and political turmoil.

For the West, too, assistance entails strains. The burdens and failures will be present and manifest. The successes and benefits will be slower and less obvious. Economic growth will not automatically produce political stability and orderly democracy. Indeed, the early effects may be more disorder and more turmoil. The proponents of assistance, in justifying the programs, have often led Congress and the public to expect too much too soon. The penalty of undue expectations has been impatience and frustration, which jeopardize support for the program. Many may feel that the task is hopeless. Others may question its wisdom or value.

In short, the efforts of the West to cooperate in modernizing the less-developed countries seem certain to be plagued indefinitely by severe frictions and tensions. The diversity in outlook, the novelty and complexity of modernizing, and the slowness of results all contribute to these conditions. In this field the components for successful policy are hard to achieve: consensus on long-term purposes, concerting of agreed programs, and steady persistence.

THE LONG-RANGE IMPACT

Earlier I suggested that the history of international affairs since World War II could be viewed as a gradual learning process. The instances I have discussed are part of that process—historic efforts to understand the existing and emerging external environment and its imperatives and constraints, and to devise and pursue suitable courses, usually with others, to modify or determine its future pattern. These are only selected instances; they do not cover the whole range of foreign policy. Even so, containment, European integration, and development assistance are major segments of our total policy. Their analysis seems to me to offer some rewarding insights into what is required for effective policies under the conditions facing us. The three instances display several common features which serve to define the problem.

On the one hand, the desired result in each case is inherently long-term; it is expected to take several decades of steady effort to achieve. Progress toward it depends on the slow process of modifying the attitudes, conceptions, and purposes of leaders, other individuals, and groups, usually by creating new or different conditions to which they might adapt their own actions.

Thus containment was designed to block Communist efforts to expand on all fronts over an indefinite period, in the belief that frustration plus internal evolution would ultimately cause them to abandon efforts at domination. Clearly success depended on the cumulative effects of actions at many points, often jointly with others. Similarly, European integration was conceived as a gradual process for creating the basis for a political community in both attitudes and institutions. The institutions of the European Community were symbols of the underlying concept and means for developing the desired relations and attitudes. The operation of the Community at each stage was expected to generate the pressures and the practical foundation for new measures. And modernizing of the less-developed countries exhibits similar features. Within each developing nation, the process entails widespread changes in attitudes, habits and institutions. Outside assistance can help to speed up this process by fostering conditions favorable to such changes and by encouraging leaders to make wise choices. But success depends on gradually modifying conduct and relations within the country.

On the other hand, the levers of change are the day-to-day actions and decisions. Under modern conditions, they cover an incredible range from crises to routine.

The dramatic crises attract the greatest attention, but focusing on their immediate danger may obscure their wider significance. Usually, crises are the outcroppings of much deeper forces, and their handling is pregnant with future consequences. The Cuban crisis of October, 1962, is an example. The Soviet missiles and forces in Cuba and the response of the United States had an import far beyond Cuba and the present. At the least the Soviets hoped to create a counter for future bargaining on Berlin or Turkish bases or other disputes. At best they might cast doubts on the resolve of the United States which could gradually erode its alliances around the world. By spreading its military mantle over Cuba, the Soviet Union sought to make good its earlier pledge to protect Communist regimes anywhere, and encourage Communists seeking power elsewhere. And Cuba itself could become a training and operations base for future Communist subversion in Latin America. Obviously, the United States reaction and the Soviet backdown affected the general prestige and influence of both.

The great mass of activities, however, are not prompted by current crises. They cover an extremely wide gamut. Global in scope, they impinge directly or subtly on the daily life of our own citizens and those of many far-off countries. To a great extent they are operational and generally entail working intimately with other nations. They may be carrying out programs established by earlier basic decisions—such as development assistance or trade negotiations. Or they may be designed to create capabilities for future actions—military, economic, political—and may require lead times as long as a decade for planning, research, development, and training of specialists.

Thus, the influence of all these activities on the ultimate outcome depends on their *cumulative* impact over time. The actions of a nation or group of nations may serve to reinforce each other, or they may cancel each other out. Which occurs depends mainly on how far these activities are governed by some pattern, how far they are organized and coordinated—both within a single government and among various governments working together. Hence continuity and consistency of policy are crucial ingredients in the process of conscious change. The influence of a nation on others, whether friendly or hostile, depends heavily on their expectations of its future conduct. Its reliability is what gives weight to its threats or promises. When the course of a strong nation is predictable, this becomes part of the "reality" for others, on which friendly nations can rely in undertaking joint activities, or to which opponents may have to adjust their own purposes and actions.

REQUISITES

In short, for a foreign policy oriented to shaping a future order, the prime problem is how to manage day-to-day decisions and operations, and concert them with those of other nations, in such a way as to advance consistently toward long-term objectives.

The requisites for conducting such a policy, I suggest, are three: 1) clarity regarding long-run objectives as a basis for general guidelines and priorities; 2) suitable intermediate programs for practical action, which will advance toward the longer goals and also enhance the capacity for future actions; 3) steadiness and patience in pursuing such goals and programs.

The first requisite is a basic conception about where we want to go. This strategy must flow from an analysis of the external environment, our own purposes and interests, and our capacity for influence. What is needed is not a blueprint—that is clearly not feasible—but general guidelines to define long-term interests, objectives, and priorities. Such long-term purposes must be solidly based on a valid appraisal of the situation and the basic forces affecting it. While the appraisal must start from conditions as they exist, the main concern should be with what they may become and how they may be modified by suitable courses of action over time. Excessive "realism" about the present has an implicit tendency to project a static future; nothing could be more misleading in times of radical change.

Moreover, in fixing long-term objectives, the truism about tailoring one's aims to capability can also be an unreliable guide, if literally applied. The relevant criterion is not merely the present ability to produce a result, but the capacity for influence over an extended period. As has been said, that capability can often be enhanced by proceeding by stages which create conditions for further action. This concept—which underlies the European Community—is a vital element in judging how situations can be gradually transformed. In other words, the crucial factor is potential capacity which may be realized or enhanced by suitable intermediate actions. In analyzing long-term alternatives, the policy-maker must try to identify and rule out those which are clearly unattainable, even by dedicated effort. But among those which appear open, his choice must recognize that the prospects for one outcome or another will be substantially affected by the policies and actions of the major protagonists. Thus he will usually be less concerned with computing the odds for a preferred course than in considering how he can improve them. The instances already discussed illuminate some of these points.

The value of an agreed strategy is clearest in the cases of containment and European integration. As those cases also indicate, the perception of a new situation and of the need to act together to meet it is greatly facilitated where the interested nations draw on common experience and background. That factor fostered the consensus of the West Europeans and the United States regarding the character of the Soviet threat. And having gone through the Hitler era and reflected on its lessons, they readily reached common judgments as to the appropriate response once the threat was identified. Common experience also operated in European integration. The Six which formed the Coal and Steel Community and the later Communities had suffered comparable ordeals in the war, and their leaders and states were predisposed to reach similar judgments as to the implications of their history, the kind of action called for, and its feasibility.

Development assistance is the converse case. The diversity in experience, history, and background between the advanced and less-developed nations has been a serious obstacle to arriving at the basis for joint action. Each side has difficulty in perceiving the world through the eyes of the other, and in finding the most effective ways of working together.

As a second component, effective policy depends on devising appropriate intermediate objectives and programs of action for pursuing the basic strategy. Such measures must combine the varied means available, and must provide for working with others. For joint effort, the separate nations must find ways to identify their common interests and to agree on measures suited to promoting them, and then join together for carrying out these measures. The obstacles to concerting effort arise from several circumstances. One is the sheer novelty of many of the problems and of the means for trying to cope with them. Another is the fact that the various nations seeking to cooperate do not perceive the world through the same lenses; the outlook of each is colored or distorted by its own special history or experience; time-lags impede the adjusting of thinking to evolving reality. Thus, it may take time and effort for nations to perceive their interests as compatible, even when they are. And, finally, the fact that nations have some common interests does not exclude genuine conflicts of other interests. But cooperation for joint purposes may necessitate subordination of these conflicting interests.

Intermediate programs therefore should serve two functions. By organizing and concerting action, they should move toward the basic objectives; and they can often facilitate further steps by fostering common perceptions and strengthened bonds. Intermediate goals and measures for joint action may be hard to arrive at, as all three instances indicate. Such programs raise the issues of greatest complexity. They also entail sacrifice and costs.

In the case of NATO, the decisions regarding strategy and forces have been a constant source of debate and friction. One cause is the changing military technology and limited experience and knowledge. Another is the disparity in influence and responsibility among the NATO members. The failure to agree on the most suitable strategy for deterrence and defense has impaired the readiness of some European members to demand added sacrifices from their citizens.

In the case of European integration the situation has been different. All the members were equally unfamiliar with the new conditions that they were trying to create. And their success depended on supporting the common purposes at some expense to short-run interests. But working together was facilitated by the institutions of the Community which could define and assert the common interests, and by the processes of the Community which have caused the members to confront its problems jointly within an agreed framework. These factors improve the prospects for joint action and for subordinating conflicting interests; but, as events testify, they cannot guarantee these results.

The making of joint programs for development assistance is much more difficult. The whole effort to accelerate development is a novel one, with limited experience to draw on. The internal problems of modernizing are baffling and so is the question of how to use external influence most effectively. Cooperation does not necessarily produce a similarity in outlook or priorities, since the outsiders cannot really confront the problems of modernizing or perceive the choices in the same terms as those directly responsible. Even so, the practice of working together does tend to narrow differences in approach and allay suspicions, and thereby enhance the capacity for constructive collaboration.

The third requisite for effective policy is continuity and persistence in pursuing the basic objectives and joint programs. This cardinal requirement tests the maturity and patience of responsible officials and citizens. The process of long-term change is bound to be slow, to operate by fits and starts, and to suffer set-backs from time to time. Since the future cannot be known with certainty, decisions must be taken on the basis of inadequate knowledge or not at all. To decide when to close the books, and act on what is known and can be surmised, calls for courage and conviction. Moreover, the pressures of crises, with allies or opponents, may tempt a political leader to sacrifice longer-term purposes for short-run gains. And, in a democracy, the general bent of the press, the political process, and public opinion is to foster impatience, frustration, and disillusion. Maintaining consistency within the government and continuity in public support, despite these pressures, is one of the chief duties for democratic leaders.

The importance of continuity of policy and the obstacles to it are displayed by the experience with containment, European integration, and modernization. Each policy inevitably has gone through periods of confusion and debate and divergence. In NATO the disputes have involved questions of strategy, forces, nuclear sharing, and the like. In the European Community, they have arisen with respect to new steps like the European Defense Community, or the entry of Britain, and now on some of the issues to be settled within the framework of the Community. In the case of the less-developed countries, criticism and impatience about shortcomings are constantly threatening to undermine the support for the assistance program.

All this underscores the importance of persistence and patience. It also points right back to the first requisite— that of identifying and agreeing on basic purposes which set the framework for policy. Clarity on the long-term objectives makes persistence and continuity more likely. In NATO, the basic conception was the necessity to pursue a policy of collective defense and deterrence. In the European Community, the basic idea was to create a Community which would transcend the parochial interests of the members and to proceed step-by-step in trying to make it a reality. In the less-developed countries, the basic objective has been slower to emerge with clarity for the reasons which I have discussed. This lack of consensus on underlying purposes both within the assisting countries and between them and the recipient countries has been one of the causes for the rather unsteady support for this program.

In the case of the other two, NATO and the European Community, the fact that the partners understood their underlying purposes aided them to cooperate in seeking intermediate programs to carry out their purposes. Because they were united on the basic purpose, they were able to keep working at these more divisive aspects of cooperation. Thus the shared perspective contributes to maintaining the constancy and patience of the partners.

In short, each of the three components—basic strategy, agreed programs, and persistence—has an important part to play in an effective policy to shape the future. All are related to the task of identifying common interests and finding ways of pursuing them jointly. And they are also valuable in maintaining the frame of mind necessary for continuous effort to transcend the inevitable obstacles to such cooperation.

This analysis obviously provides no short-cut for the creation of an order congenial to free societies. The hard necessity to comprehend the emerging environment, to define valid long-term objectives, to organize diverse actions, and to pursue them with steady patience poses staggering challenges, both intellectual and operational. The grueling effort to meet them will be evoked only by awareness that they are the requisites for effective policy-making.

2

The Search for an
Atlantic Order

In constructing a world order congenial to freedom and diversity, the Atlantic nations must provide the foundations. Their own security and prosperity depend on working together on many fronts. Their concerted help is essential to provide the capital and markets desperately needed by the modernizing societies of Asia, Africa, and Latin America. Their strength must maintain the major bulwark against Communist expansion. And only if faced with a unified West will Soviet coexistence gradually evolve into genuine efforts for secure peace.

Together the Atlantic nations can produce adequate resources, both human and material, to cope with these complex and stubborn problems. Their shared traditions and values and their advanced economies provide the bases for shaping the emerging order, if they combine their efforts.

The crucial question is how the West organizes itself. What shall be the structure of Europe? How shall it be related to the United States? The answers will determine whether the Atlantic nations mobilize or dissipate their capacity to influence the future.

For nearly a decade and a half, the shared goals have been to build a strong integrated Europe linked in partnership with the United States for the pursuit of common purposes. These twin aims are firmly rooted in hard experience.

In Europe, as we have seen, two civil wars had certified the necessity for a new structure solid enough to assure stability and well-being. Such a structure could not be built on the classic pattern of cooperation among sovereign states, concerting national policy by unanimity. A new order in Europe demanded the strong frame of an integrated community. Franco-German rivalry could be transcended only in the creative task of building a united Europe, which would weave together vital interests and offer a wide arena for the energies of the people. For the permanent benefits of an enlarged market, more was required than removal of trade barriers; there must be an economic union, with mobility for labor, capital, and enterprise, and with common policies for agriculture, transport, and other fields. To have a major voice in a world of super-powers, Europe would have to act as a unit in mobilizing resources and using its influence in foreign affairs and defense.

To attain these ends would call ultimately for a European political entity with power to govern within vital but limited fields entrusted to it by the member nations. This quasi-federal Europe could be approached only step-by-step by partial stages. But if it fulfills its promise, the European Community will be a watershed in the long history of Europe and a new great power comparable in population and industrial base to the United States and the Soviet Union.

From the time of the Marshall Plan, the United States has given firm, bipartisan support to European unity. In both its aims and its methods, the movement for European integration appealed to the American temper and outlook. As President Kennedy said at Philadelphia on July 4, 1962, "the basic objective of our foreign policy for seventeen years" has been to aid the progress toward a strong and united Europe. "We see in such a Europe a partner with whom we could deal on a basis of full equality in all the great and burdensome tasks of building and defending a community of free nations."

And the need for a united Europe to be an equal partner was the main theme of the President's trip to Europe in June, 1963. This steady American support, like the European Community itself, has its origin in the lessons of practical experience, experience that had taught the necessity for the Atlantic nations to work together for security, prosperity, and external purposes. Besides defense, in the words of Jean Monnet: "There are urgent problems which neither Europe nor America can settle alone. These are to my mind the monetary stability of the West, the organization of agriculture in an increasingly industrial world, help to the developing countries to speed their growth, and of course, the freeing of trade to be negotiated between yourselves and the Common Market."

And experience had also shown how seriously collaboration was impeded by the wide gulf in power, responsibility, and outlook between the United States and the separate states of Europe. In his Paulskirche speech in June, 1963, the President stressed the point: "Only such a [fully cohesive] Europe will permit full reciprocity of treatment across the ocean, in facing the Atlantic agenda. With only such a Europe can we have a full give-and-take between equals, an equal sharing of responsibilities, and an equal level of sacrifice."

Thus the European Community and Atlantic partnership complement each other. Each is essential to complete the other. Both are necessary to enable the Atlantic nations to meet their urgent needs and responsibilities at home and abroad.

This creative effort to organize the West has been under way for over a decade. In that period, as we have seen, much has been achieved toward the long-term goals within Europe and in the Atlantic area. Early in 1963, this steady progress was interrupted and the outlook put in doubt. The direct cause of the current cleavages is

General de Gaulle and his policies. But Europe and the Atlantic alliance are also subject to other strains which he has intensified and exploited.

This situation offers an intriguing chance for analysis in the terms discussed in the last chapter. The Community and partnership constitute a long-term strategy for organizing an Atlantic structure. Over the last decade these basic objectives have inspired and guided specific programs for pursuing them. The progress of the European Community has created a new situation which generates new forces and new problems. In examining the current stage in this process, I will focus mainly on the interaction with British policy, United States-European relations, and de Gaulle's policies. Then I will suggest some conclusions about courses for dealing with this situation.

THE UNITED KINGDOM

For Britain, the progress of the European Community forced a belated revision of major premises of her policy. From 1950 to 1961 she consistently rejected any part in an integrated Europe. In 1950, the Labour government stayed out of the Coal and Steel Community. Shortly afterward, the Conservative government declined to join in forming the European Defense Community. From 1955 to 1957, when the European Economic Community and the Euratom were being worked out, Britain again held aloof. Then, on August 9, 1961, she requested talks with the Six on the terms for her entry into the Communities.

Thus for eleven years, the policy of Britain was based on premises about Europe and her relations to it and to the world which proved ill-founded. The reasons for this time-lag and for the ultimate reversal of policy offer instructive insights into the process of adjusting a nation's outlook and objectives to changed conditions.

In fairness it is essential to keep in mind that the change in the British position has been an extreme one. As late as 1907 Sir Eyre Crowe, in a famous memorandum, had analyzed British policy in terms which conceived of Britain as the center of the international order. The bases of British policy were her command of the seas, her empire, plus her role as balancer in the European balance of power. After World War II, all this clearly lay in the past. The last stage in four decades of declining power was the dismantling of the Empire. Britain did modify her concept of her role. She took an active part in OEEC, the Brussels Pact, and NATO. But her limited revision fell far short of that made by the Continental powers.

Many factors impeded a more radical reappraisal of the British position. Britain had not, of course, suffered the defeat and collapse in World War II which, on the

Continent, had produced disillusion with the national state and nationalism. Indeed, the victory, won by sacrifice and courage, had revived a sense of British identity and purpose. Then, in the postwar period, Britain continued to stress the "special relation" with the United States, forged in the conduct of the war. The links of language, history, and values were still close. But the situation was not the same. With her heavy dependence on the United States, Britain was no longer an equal partner. Sentiment helped to cloud the reality. Wishful thinking about Britain's position was also encouraged by the existence of the Commonwealth. During the war, the empire and the Commonwealth were major components of British strength. In the postwar world, this too changed when the empire, in India and Africa, was converted into independent nations, within the Commonwealth. While useful as a point of contact, the Commonwealth was no substitute for the empire as a source of real strength. But again, the appearance hid the reality. The Commonwealth, with its vast population, inflated the apparent power and influence of Britain.

The tradition of British foreign policy also inhibited reappraisal. In his volume on diplomacy, Harold Nicolson comments that "for the last hundred years British statesmen have done their best to avoid any planned or long-term foreign policy and to eschew as far as possible all precise continental commitments." [1] European integration offended this tradition in two ways: it was a long-term plan and it was a permanent commitment to Europe. British thinking resisted both. In fact, Britain expected European integration to fail. In British eyes, such long-term projections in the future were grandiose. They were paper schemes, not practical measures.

With these premises, British leaders sought to retain an independent role in world affairs. With her various assets, Britain could be a link within three circles of power: the Commonwealth, the Atlantic alliance, especially the United States, and the Europe of OEEC and the Council of Europe. This framework, she felt, allowed her considerable room for freedom of action and independent influence. To join the European Community would jeopardize this position to no advantage.

Unfortunately, the foundations were not solid enough to support this policy. Thus the United Kingdom misjudged its potentialities and its real alternatives. But a decade passed before Britain's leaders recognized this harsh fact by the decision of mid-1961 to seek entry into the Community. The delay was costly.

During the 1950s, British policy hindered the movement to European integration. The European Defense

[1] Harold Nicolson, *Diplomacy* (New York, Harcourt, Brace, 1939), p. 136.

Community might have been approved by France, if Britain had been a full member or even had extended to EDC the commitments she later made to the Western European Union. In 1956–57, Britain greatly complicated the Common Market negotiations by her Free Trade Area proposals. In 1959, she formed the EFTA largely to bring pressure on the European Community. And to bolster her independent role Britain developed her national nuclear capabilities.

The European Community went forward despite British policy. Indeed, its growing success was the main factor in the British decision to enter. By 1961, its impact was already substantial and its import even greater. Economically Britain was concerned with being outside the Common Market. And politically the Community threatened to dwarf any separate role for Britain, especially as the Commonwealth and the "special relation" came to be seen with greater realism.

This episode teaches a lesson important for our discussion. In 1950, and at each new stage of the European Community, its proponents, who were then eager for the British to participate, faced a choice. They could either proceed without her or attempt to bring her in by watering down the Community. They went ahead in the conviction that Britain would change her position only when the Community had become an operating reality which she could not ignore. The EDC setback delayed this process, by seeming to justify doubts about integration. But by pushing ahead to create the Community, the Six did make it necessary for Britain to revise her policy.

The British slowness in changing her policy, however, made the efforts for her entry far more complex. Many of the problems were inherently hard to solve, but the formation of EFTA had added complications. And so did the fact that the Community was now a going concern of nearly four years. Special arrangements to ease particular British problems could not be conceded so readily as could have been done at the formation of the Community. The timing of the negotiations also forced the Six to settle among themselves ahead of schedule some of the more delicate issues involved in carrying out their treaty. On both sides, negotiating positions tended to be rigid: for the Six because they had to be reached by compromises among themselves; and for Britain because any concession was likely to offend some segment of the Cabinet or the party or the electorate, just when the government's popular standing was declining, and younger ministers must have been jockeying for positions within the party. Given this situation, the negotiations were inevitably extremely cautious and protracted. That in turn imposed further strains on the Community and interfered with its progress toward political integration. The extremely limited proposals of the Fouchet Committee for consultation, for example, were opposed by the Dutch lest they impede British entry.

Even after 1961, the course of Britain was confusing to many. The government apparently wanted to enter the Community, but did not carry on an active campaign to obtain public support for entry or admit its political implications. The debate in the Commonwealth was not helpful. During the negotiations, the Labour Party decided in effect to oppose entry and to make the issue a party one. Even so, leaders in business, the press, and government appeared to be convinced that Britain must take an active role in Europe, join the Community, and adjust her other relations accordingly. Of some hundred intellectuals queried by the magazine *Encounter*, for example, about three quarters favored British entry with the rest divided evenly between opposition and indecision.

Yet the handling of the nuclear issue at Nassau and after showed that the British government still hankered for an independent role. Just as in the 1950s, it justified a British nuclear force as the means to independent influence in world affairs. The debates in the Commons highlighted the ambiguous attitude of Macmillan and many of his ministers as to the future role of Britain.

Delay and doubt played into the hands of de Gaulle. Having settled the Algerian issue, the General had had time to solidify his domestic position by the referendum and election in late 1962. And his firm grasp on France allowed him much greater latitude to pursue his views on the future of Europe. Some of those views were soon revealed at his press conference in January, 1963, breaking off the negotiations with Britain, essentially for political reasons. But for his action, Britain would almost certainly have joined the Community. There were still problems to resolve, but as the subsequent report of the Commission indicates, these could have been worked out with good will.

De Gaulle's veto will test the tenacity of the British in seeking to join. While her present predicament will cause some awkward problems for Britain and others, these effects should not be disastrous even if her entry is delayed several years. Indefinite exclusion from the Community, however, would surely have profound effects on British attitudes and policies. In any case the situation highlights the necessity for Britain to clarify its own aims and priorities.

THE COMMUNITY AS A PARTNER

For relations between the United States and Europe, the current stage of European integration creates serious strains.

As Europe has revived, its people have recovered their self-confidence and pride. The Europeans are keenly aware how radically the situation of Europe relative to the United States has shifted since the extreme postwar disparity. In growth rates and levels of economic activity, the Community has far surpassed the United States over the last decade. With monetary reserves rivaling ours, surpluses of the Community now contrast with our persistent deficits in the balance of payments. For many, especially those under forty, the Community has already made "Europe" a reality and fostered a sense of being "European." De Gaulle's actions may jeopardize the progress of the Community, but they often capitalize on these European feelings.

This resurgent Europe deeply wants a more self-respecting role in the world. This desire is already strong and will steadily become stronger. In particular, the Europeans wish to redress the balance with the United States. Their present role does not seem to reflect the changes of the last decade or to be in keeping with their relative strength. The sense of being a ward of the United States is offensive to many Europeans, whatever their gratitude for past help.

While this pressure is expressed in various ways, much of it has centered on the nuclear field. With enhanced confidence, the European members want a larger place in planning NATO strategy and in control over the forces for its defense, especially nuclear. The steady growth of Soviet nuclear weapons and missiles has, of course, brought the nuclear issue to the fore. Even so, most Europeans appear to realize that if necessary the United States would assuredly use its nuclear capacity for the defense of Europe. Indeed their confidence that the Soviets are and will be deterred from any attack on Europe leads them to resist U.S. proposals for modifying NATO strategy. But the issue of nuclear control is not primarily military; it has become symbolic of standing or dependence.

The European aspiration for a larger role—for greater equality with the United States—has outrun their present capacity to fulfill it. Despite its potential, Europe cannot yet act as a "great power." No European entity now exists in most fields, including defense and foreign policy. Thus the new self-confidence and sense of growing power in Europe cannot find an effective outlet; they therefore are often expressed in resistance to U.S. leadership.

Here is the crux of the problem faced by American policy toward Europe at this stage: the Europe which would be a full partner is only emergent, yet the Europeans want and expect to be treated as equal partners already. This dilemma appears in many guises.

Almost any major issue affecting the Alliance or its members highlights the existing disparity. Thus, when NATO tries to cope with strategy, the other members feel overwhelmed; and lacking data or background to take an effective part, they resist initiatives of the United States, and, in some cases, interpret them to impugn its resolve. In negotiations with the Soviet Union, or at the United Nations, when the role of the United States is inevitably central, its efforts to consult its allies or keep them informed cannot wholly compensate for the feeling that their interests are in the hands of others.

And some courses of the United States, especially toward Britain, have blurred the real choices for the European nations. During the 1950s, it would have been inappropriate to pressure Britain into casting her lot with an integrated Europe. But has it been wise or helpful to allow the "special relation" to bolster an outdated image of her influence and options? Doing so surely delayed reappraisal of her situation. Doubtless the adjustment would have been painfully slow in any case, but so much the more reason for not retarding it. In this light, renewing assistance for a British atomic force in 1958 was an unfortunate decision, and so was the Nassau Agreement to prolong the British national deterrent with Polaris. Both decisions cut directly across the more basic objective of fostering a united Europe for an effective partnership. No alchemy can make the separate nations of Europe—with individual resources of 10 to 12 percent of ours—into equal partners with us. The great disservice of our relation with Britain has been to nurture the illusion that somehow this could be done.

Only as the European Community becomes a more cohesive entity with wider competence will Europe enhance its capacity for effective action and equality. Until then, no devices will resolve the stresses resulting from disparity. But, if there is no cure for these tensions, more can be done to alleviate them. The NATO decisions to expand the allied share in nuclear planning and the proposed multilateral force are directed to that purpose. The NATO machinery for concerting policy, developing strategy, and combining the two could be improved materially. And the United States could doubtless be more alert to allied sensibilities than sometimes in the past. It will be wise to recognize, however, that at best tensions will persist until Europe closes the gap between aspiration and capability. Building toward equal partnership despite these strains will test patience and faith on both sides of the Atlantic.

THE POLICIES OF GENERAL DE GAULLE

For General de Gaulle, the Community offers leverage for achieving different aims. His policies challenge the very objective of constructing an integrated Europe and an Atlantic partnership.

Since the war, the primary aim of de Gaulle has been to achieve greater status and independence for a France overshadowed by the United States and the Soviet Union. His restless search for the means has led him down many paths. Since 1944, de Gaulle has, in the words of one writer, "envisaged the following alliances: with the British in order to create an independent bloc vis-à-vis the Russians and the Americans; with the Soviet Union in order to maintain an independent France; with all against the revival of a unified militarized and strong Germany; with West Germany and the West European states in order to create an independent bloc —a Third Force in Europe." [2]

General de Gaulle's attitude toward the European Community flows from his concepts as to the role of France. For him the ultimate reality is the sovereign nation-state—and above all France. His vision of European unity is based on coordinating policies among sovereign states—a "Europe of states"—for "it is only the states that are valid, legitimate and capable of achievement." The idea of transferring authority to European institutions is anathema to him, as he has made clear many times. In his television address of April 19, 1963, for example, he said: [3] "If the union of Western Europe . . . is a capital aim in our action outside, we have no desire to be dissolved within it. Any system that would consist of handing over our sovereignty to supernational assemblies would be incompatible with

[2] Roy C. Macridis, "De Gaulle's Foreign Policy and the Fifth Republic," *Yale Review,* L (Winter, 1961), 178–79.

[3] English text from French Embassy Release, French Affairs, No. 154 (1963).

the rights and duties of the French Republic." Initially, he sought to revise the existing Community treaties to reduce the authority of the independent Commissions and suspended this effort only when the other members strongly opposed it.

De Gaulle wants a Europe concerted under French leadership, without sacrificing the relative independence of France. Basically he aspires to use Europe's revised strength to foster and expand French influence. Similarly, he rejects the idea of Atlantic partnership, which he depicts as a device for perpetuating American hegemony over Europe. His goal is an independent Europe dealing at arm's length with the United States and the Soviet Union. While accepting the NATO umbrella, he opposes integration of defense forces under SHAPE and other NATO commands. Undermining American influence in Europe will facilitate substitution of French leadership for it. That is why, *inter alia,* he must create distrust of the American deterrent and broader purposes.

The General can hardly assume that other Europeans would embrace his concept of Europe eagerly. But his hope is to exploit existing desires to erect a sort of pyramid of power, with France at the top.

First, the close ties with West Germany provide his starting point. Indeed the German proxy is central to his strategy. To get it, he has played upon the yearning for a reconciled France and Germany by means of the recent Franco-German treaty and symbolic exchanges of visits. And he has played on Adenauer's suspicions, by using the issues of Berlin and NATO strategy to cast doubts on U.S. reliability in protecting German interests and in the defense of Europe.

Second, de Gaulle clearly intends to utilize the European Community for his purposes. The Community offers real benefits to France, in wider markets for French farmers and in aid to the associated African states, mainly former French colonies, where France retains major commercial and other interests. The others of the Six are firmly committed to the Community for both economic and political reasons. De Gaulle is counting on their desire to preserve the Community to keep them in line despite his unilateral actions. Thus in his eyes, the Economic Community, linking the members together in interdependence, offers an instrument for French leverage.

Third, de Gaulle is turning to his account the revived self-confidence of Europe. In effect, he seeks to capitalize on the European desire to regain greater control over its destiny and to adjust the balance between the United States and Europe. In "standing up to the United States" he expects to arouse and appeal to an incipient European nationalism and to enhance the influence of France.

The position of de Gaulle on nuclear issues is related to this strategy. The French national nuclear force has been justified as necessary to protect France and Europe from Soviet threats or attack as the United States becomes more vulnerable. With approaching nuclear balance, the French force, though tiny, is to deter the Soviets when the United States would not. The case does not seem convincing, even for France. If France needs her national force because allies cannot be trusted, logic would require each European nation to provide its own nuclear striking force. The French, however, do not carry the argument to its logical end. De Gaulle has not proposed that West Germany, which is more exposed than France, should acquire a national nuclear force.

The reason, I suggest, is clear. For de Gaulle, the French nuclear force is primarily a political instrument. Indeed, his independent course reflects his confidence that American nuclear strength guarantees European security. His nuclear force is designed to justify the French claim to be the leader in Europe. This symbol of primacy is to distinguish her from Germany, which undertook in 1954 not to produce such weapons, and Italy, which can hardly spare the resources. Hence arguments about the military weakness or futility of the French nuclear force, however well founded, are not likely to modify de Gaulle's program.

It is also apparent why de Gaulle blocked British

entry into the Community. The main reason for his veto was to prevent Britain from competing with France for the leadership of Europe. And he also recognized that Britain would oppose his efforts to divide Europe from the United States.

These then seem to be the strands of de Gaulle's policy for achieving an independent Europe under French leadership. The most immediate question is: how will his policy affect the European Community and the alliance?

The unilateral action of de Gaulle in January, 1963, checked the momentum of the Community. Its progress had been speeded by the confidence of the members that the Community was genuinely a common enterprise with shared aims. On that basis, sacrifices of local or parochial interests, required for each new step, could be justified in domestic politics as serving the larger political purposes of ending rivalries in Europe, creating a prosperous economy, and enhancing Europe's influence on its own destiny. De Gaulle's action impaired this attitude.

The impartial Commission of the Community, in its first statement to the European Assembly after the breakdown of negotiations, made this point quite explicitly. It said: "Our Community has been faced with its first real crisis. . . . The crisis is one of confidence, and that is what makes it so serious. The life of our Community depends upon everyone looking upon and treating Community matters as matters of real joint responsibility. . . . It is also necessary to avoid creating the impression that the Community and its aims, the Community institutions, and the Community procedure are merely instruments of one country's diplomacy."

This crisis of confidence could jeopardize the future of the Community. Under the treaty, Council action will be required to move ahead in working out programs of the Community in many fields. The feeling that one member treats the Community as a lever for its own purposes would seriously impair the ability to resolve such issues. And if the Community should falter, business firms which have been investing and planning on the premise that the Community would become effective, probably ahead of schedule, would probably postpone action with profound effects on the outlook for the Community.

In view of de Gaulle's attitude, a revival of momentum may be extremely slow. While doubt remains, the other members will at least insist that in any new steps benefits and burdens be balanced—or "synchronized" in the words of Foreign Minister Schroeder at the Community Ministers meeting on April 27, 1963. But a shift merely to a "trading" basis, normal in relations among states, could gradually erode the Community approach which has been the unique feature of progress thus far.

De Gaulle's basic outlook poses an even graver danger to the new edifice in Europe. His deep faith in the nation-state as the ultimate reality could lead to undoing all that has been achieved since 1950. The other members of the European Community, including Germany after Adenauer, will not accept French predominance of the sort de Gaulle has in mind. If he persists in his course, however, he may well revive the nationalism and outmoded rivalries which so many have dedicated themselves to wipe out. If Europe reverts to its historic pattern of nation-states competing for primacy, it is surely not inevitable that France would prevail. What is certain is that the result for Europe and the West would be a tragic betrayal of the most creative enterprise since World War II. The outcome of de Gaulle's policy could be to demonstrate once more the bitter consequences of a misguided reversion to the past.

De Gaulle could also do grave damage to the alliance. The French, under de Gaulle, appear to be engaged in a systematic effort to throw suspicion on American reliability. Every action of the United States to modify NATO strategy, to assure closer control of nuclear weapons, to provide a wider range of responses, has been depicted as designed to disengage the United States from the defense of Europe. This campaign has had some effects already and may have more as time goes on. It is far easier to erode the cement of confidence among allies than it is to repair the damage. And distrust could later weaken the ability of the alliance to withstand Soviet threats or blackmail.

The design of General de Gaulle would therefore negate the long-term goal of a unified Europe acting as a partner of the United States for constructive purposes. His Europe would not be an integrated community but a coalition of states led by France. His Europe would not be a partner of the United States but as independent and separate as possible. It would be unwise to gloss over this direct clash in basic aims. Thus de Gaulle's policy demands a clear answer.

THE ANSWER TO GENERAL DE GAULLE

In these circumstances, the sound course is to press ahead with constructing the European Community and Atlantic partnership. The needs which prompted these long-term objectives have not diminished. Not to oppose the efforts of de Gaulle to thwart these basic aims would be folly. It is essential to assure that the European Community is not subverted into an instrument of French predominance, and that Europe and the United States are not divided to the damage of both.

Some seem to cherish the hope that the General can be wheedled into compromising his objectives or be weaned away from them by concessions. That view hardly does justice to de Gaulle. He is not a man who can be coaxed or bribed to change his policies. Concessions to that end would be most ill-advised. He will only use them to advance his own purposes.

But that does not mean that his objectives cannot be changed. As Algeria showed, brute facts can cause him to modify his plans. The problem is to make sure that events convince him that his concept of Europe will not succeed. The United States and its European partners are not without means to influence the environment of General de Gaulle. His course seems out of keeping with the basic forces of our time. De Gaulle is, in reality, clinging to the nationalism which the Community aims to transcend. His French nationalism excludes the integrated Europe which would be essential for the independent European role he desires. The other Europeans will not accept French hegemony. And the independent course he seeks for Europe will not serve its interests. De Gaulle's power is negative—the ability to veto, to divide, and to destroy. Given the interdependence of the Atlantic nations, this power affords considerable leverage if used as ruthlessly as de Gaulle seems ready to do. But strong bases exist for concerted action to lead de Gaulle to recognize the necessity to revise his plans.

Whether this can be done will depend as much on the Europeans as on the United States. In the European Community, only the Commission and the other members can assure that the Community goes forward without allowing France to twist it to its parochial purposes. Only the United Kingdom can ultimately decide whether to work imaginatively for future adhesion to Europe.

Much turns on the attitude of the Federal Republic. Without German support, the position of de Gaulle would be drastically changed. De Gaulle has no interest in going it alone. As he recognizes, France by itself simply does not have the power to conduct a policy such as he envisages. Everything depends on being able to speak in the name of Europe, and for that he needs the firm backing of the Federal Republic in order to pull along the other members of the Six.

With Adenauer gone, de Gaulle's influence on German policy is likely to decline; the successors of the Chancellor, while anxious for French friendship, do not seem inclined to lend themselves to de Gaulle's purposes. Their handling of the Franco-German treaty is an encouraging sign. By adding the preamble, the Bundestag and the major parties recorded their insistence that German-French relations be managed so as to reinforce the European Community, NATO, and Atlantic partnership, and to facilitate ultimate British entry into the Community. Of course, their attitude could change, especially if German concerns or interests should be treated casually in Western negotiations with the Soviets. This factor certainly weighed heavily with Adenauer and could even drive his successors into de Gaulle's arms.

The policies and actions of the United States will also be crucial for their influence both on de Gaulle and on the course of its European partners, especially in the period ahead with the new leadership in Germany, an unsteady Italian government, and British policy in flux. The vital thing is to see that our actions do not enhance, but erode, the leverage of de Gaulle. We must fully recognize the reality of the European feelings which he seeks to exploit and the effect of our attitude on his ability to do so.

The United States will have to do more to show its readiness to work with Europe as a partner. Admittedly, as I have said, this is not easy to do while an effective European entity does not exist for foreign affairs, defense, and other fields. But the creation of the partnership cannot await a completed European Community. Like the Community, the partnership will have to develop by stages and evolve in step with it. As part of the process the United States will have to adjust its thinking to the import of a real partnership. As a nation, our attitudes still reflect much of the heritage of the postwar dependence of Europe. We have not absorbed what it must mean to share responsibility in monetary and economic policy, in defense, in agricultural programs, and many other fields. In short, interdependence, while talked about, is not yet grasped as a practical restraint on our own freedom of action. In the period ahead, it would contribute to the prospects for both the European Community and Atlantic partnership if the United States could convey by its actions a greater awareness of what sharing responsibility with Europe will imply for both sides.

COURSES WITHIN THE COMMUNITY

Within the European Community, the primary effort of the other Five should be to reassert and reinforce the concept of a truly integrated Europe.

In going forward with the Common Market they can require the French to reciprocate for benefits received at each stage. Thus the Five may well try to use agriculture as a lever for getting French cooperation in the 1964 GATT trade negotiations arising from the Trade Expansion Act. The agriculture program is of special interest to the French, who hope to expand their output and markets within the Community. In his July, 1963, press conference, de Gaulle virtually threatened to stall the Common Market unless the farm program was worked out by a deadline of December 31, 1963. This program will impose serious burdens on the high-cost German farmers, who will be gradually squeezed out.

The Germans, however, are more eager than the French for success in the trade negotiations in GATT, which will, of course, depend heavily on the positions taken by the Community. Thus, there may be the makings of a constructive "package deal," with the French agreeing to cooperate on the GATT negotiations in return for acceptable Community solutions for agriculture. Such an outcome may be encouraged by the fact that after 1966, no member of the Community will be able, under the treaty, to block tariff cuts or a farm program desired by the other members.

As a second course, the Five could well launch a new initiative for political integration. Various steps proposed at earlier stages might be revived. The separate Commissions for Coal and Steel, the Common Market, and Euratom could well be merged into a single Commission for the Community, exercising the existing powers under the various treaties. The Fouchet plan for political consultation could be reopened as a basis for concerting in foreign affairs and later in defense. The members of the European Parliament, now appointed from national Parliaments, could be elected by popular franchise, as the treaties envision. The revenues from the agricultural levies, and perhaps from the common external tariff, might be allocated to the Community with the European Parliament having the authority to appropriate them for Community purposes.

All of these, and similar measures, would require French approval to become effective. This may well be refused, but it is not certain. The other Five have considerable leverage on de Gaulle if they stand together. But even if France blocks action, it is highly desirable to define the issue clearly as to what is to be the character of the Community.

THE NUCLEAR ISSUE

The nuclear issue has become a sort of touchstone in the relations between the United States and the European members of NATO. The NATO actions at Ottawa were a sign of the ferment within the alliance. The various measures—the SHAPE deputy for nuclear matters, the NATO liaison group at SAC headquarters to plan targeting, even the so-called inter-allied force (though largely a formal change)—should be useful in drawing other NATO members into nuclear planning. These steps should be pursued and developed.

But they do not get to the heart of the matter. Increasingly Europeans feel that sharing in nuclear control is the mark of first-class status. Most recognize that the defense of the Atlantic area is a single problem and that a strategic nuclear war would involve both Europe and the United States. But until the Atlantic area is a single political unit, there is a dilemma—Europeans are not likely to be satisfied for the long run with a solution leaving all decisions to the President, and making them wards of the United States indefinitely. If they are to be partners in defense, they expect to share the ultimate right to utilize such weapons for their defense. In practice, it is very hard to envisage a case where the Europeans would wish to use such weapons when the United States would not be ready to do so. But the right to do so may well be highly important in terms of self-respect. The United States, for many good reasons, might prefer to keep unified control of these weapons. But in practice that does not seem a genuine option.

The critical question is how to handle this issue so as to contribute to European unity and Atlantic partnership and not fragment them. In seeking an answer, it is essential to recognize that no solution which is feasible now or soon will fully satisfy the desirable criteria. The situation is not yet ripe for any final answer. Attitudes and conditions will have to evolve much further before a fully satisfactory resolution is attainable. Hence any suggested course for current action will be open to objection if measured by the ideal or by the desires of some protagonists. The proper tests for any proposal should be: does it point toward a constructive solution in keeping with the basic European and Atlantic objectives? Will it foster changes in conditions and attitudes which will facilitate moving toward that solution by stages? Fortunately, as we work toward an answer, the American nuclear umbrella relieves us from great urgency in military terms, and allows time for development. But politically, because of the British and French efforts for one thing, the issue cannot be evaded.

Among many variants, the ultimate choice is between national nuclear forces in Europe and some form of integrated force—either European or Atlantic. With the objective clarified, there is then the question of what practical steps can be taken now to move toward it.

National European forces seriously jeopardize the more basic objectives. They are bound to be wasteful of resources, ineffective as deterrents, and divisive of Europe and the alliance. Of these, the political damage seems most serious. In justifying their national forces, both British and French leaders have insisted that they are necessary for the ultimate security of the nation and to avoid being a satellite of the United States. If that is constantly asserted, it would be rash to assume that political leaders of the Federal Republic, Italy, and perhaps other members will not sooner or later be driven to seek similar forces for their nations. Many Germans say frankly that they cannot accept a second-class status within the alliance indefinitely. National German nuclear forces would impose severe strains on the alliance; but continued inequality will be likely to do so as well. The objections to national forces apply to the British force as well as to the French. The United States has been right in not helping the French force, and should continue to refrain from assistance. But it was a mistake at Nassau to give a new lease on life to the British nuclear force.

These objections are not met by the so-called inter-allied nuclear force suggested by the British at Nassau and approved at the NATO meeting at Ottawa in 1963. That step does little more than put a NATO label over existing forces, leaving them operationally under national command and control. This scheme may foster more joint planning and targeting, but it has crippling limitations. Under it the national components can always be pulled out, in a military crisis or for political reasons, which could undermine joint planning. And it seems to legitimize national nuclear forces without solving the problem of discrimination or duplication. In theory, national units could be welded into a unified joint force with effective safeguards to prevent withdrawal. In practice, such complete and final surrender of national control would be incompatible with the asserted reasons for national forces. Besides, even such measures would not cure the disparity in status among different allies and control would raise intractible issues regarding national veto over use.

It has also been proposed that the United States should aid the French and British national forces as a route to a European force. How it would lead there is not explained. This proposal also suffers from defects already discussed. Aiding national forces will only justify their asserted rationale. De Gaulle has shown no interest in giving up control of the French force; he would use such help to advance his own aims, which could readily undermine the alliance and the European Community. The support for French and British forces would underscore the different status of Germany and others and exacerbate the strains already mentioned. Thus, such a course would offer little prospect of leading to a joint European force. Indeed, it seems more likely to defeat such an objective.

This leaves the possibility of a genuincly unified multilateral force. Such a force would not be made up of national components but would be truly integrated with mixed-manning and joint ownership and control by the participants. For many reasons a seaborne force seems a desirable way to start. Such a force, whether ultimately Atlantic or European, offers many advantages.

Unlike national forces, it would not fragment the alliance but should tend to pull it together. By joint effort, the members can create a respectable force without unduly diverting resources from conventional capabilities. And such a force would enable the Federal Republic to have a proper part in the control of nuclear defense without raising the spectre of separate German strategic forces.

Undoubtedly such an integrated force would pose some hard practical problems. The questions of manning, training, and operating are not so difficult as they first appear. Competent naval experts who have studied these problems seriously are confident that they can be solved for surface ships or submarines. They consider that a force manned by mixed crews can be fully effective as a fighting instrument.

The problem of control is inevitably complex as long as Europe is not a cohesive political unit. The solution would have to be geared to an evolving context over eight to ten years. During the coming decade Europe may well advance toward an effective entity; and its relations with the United States will evolve. Some four or five years at least would be required to create an integrated force and to put it into operation. Initially, control could be handled by some form of committee, with advance decisions to govern use of the force in the clearest cases, such as direct nuclear attack on the

NATO area. Thus it would be feasible to start the formation of an integrated force without waiting to settle the final form of control; a decade or more would be available to work out a definitive system in the light of developing conditions.

This fact does not, however, justify evading the crucial question: Should the United States be prepared to accept a control system which could permit the use of the integrated force without its consent? In answering the question, we do not start from a *tabula rasa*. The United States has no prospect of retaining a monopoly of the control of nuclear weapons. As now planned, the French force will be wholly under French control. In the Nassau Agreement, the United States recognized that Britain would be free to use its Polaris force in extreme national emergencies.

An integrated force offers the only alternative which avoids the expansion of national forces, with all its disadvantages. But if it were to be subject indefinitely to American veto, it could hardly achieve its political aim or encourage the future merger into it of separate national forces. In my view, therefore, as Europe moves toward unity, the United States should be willing to concede to a European or NATO force ultimate autonomy without a veto. To do so would merely extend to such an integrated force what was conceded to the British force in the Nassau agreement.

There remains the question of how such a force might be begun, given the state of affairs in Europe. The most obvious way would have been for the British to have taken the initiative. Instead of pursuing the mirage of an independent force, they could have offered to pool their resources with the other members of the European Community in creating an integrated nuclear force, which could have been targeted or operated together with American forces. Such a proposal would have converted their nuclear means into a real political asset. Britain could thereby have demonstrated beyond doubt that she was ready to devote her energies and special means to building a strong Europe. And if de Gaulle had refused to participate, that would have shown how hollow are his own claims to represent Europe. But British leadership has not been up to imaginative action of this kind.

Since 1960, the United States has stated its readiness to support a seaborne multilateral missile force. First suggested to NATO by Secretary Herter in 1960, it was reaffirmed by President Kennedy in May, 1961. And in 1962 and 1963, a U.S. team explored the concept with various NATO nations and made available technical studies for solving the various problems. The Federal Republic and Italy expressed the desire to go forward. The ultimate British position is uncertain. The debates in the British Parliament after Nassau showed remarkably limited enthusiasm for the independent British deterrent. Labour is pledged to end it, though uncommitted as to its course on a multilateral force. Under General de Gaulle, France will not participate at present.

Under these conditions, the United States would have to be a charter member if the force is to be started in the near future. But as the force evolved, and the veto on use ended in favor of some other control formula, the United States could either continue on as a member or let the force become European. In either case the aim should be to coordinate this force with the nuclear forces of the United States in planning, targeting, and in other ways.

The existence of such a multilateral force could serve as a rallying point for those in France and Britain who oppose national forces. There is a good prospect that the British force might later be merged into it as the V-Bombers became obsolete. In France, rising expense and delay may gradually create pressures like those in Britain. Even according to present French plans, almost a decade will be needed to produce their three nuclear submarines, which leaves ample time for a gradual shift in policy.

The multilateral force concept has aroused sharp attack and even ridicule. Its initial form is doubtless not the final answer. But any proposal can be seriously evaluated only by comparison with available alternatives. By that standard, the integrated force, whether ultimately

European or Atlantic, seems the most constructive course among those now feasible. It seeks to meet the problems facing us in a way which will best advance the basic aims for European unity and Atlantic partnership.

THE LOWERING OF TRADE BARRIERS

The impending Kennedy round of tariff negotiations in GATT is also significant for the Atlantic partnership.

They are important, of course, for relations between the United States and Europe. Tariff cuts will affect terms of trade and competition, the balance of payments, and agriculture. And the handling of the negotiations will bear on developing closer working bases on the two sides of the Atlantic.

But the negotiations will have a wider impact. They will reveal to some extent how far the Atlantic nations are ready and able to cooperate in tackling problems affecting other regions of the world. As the negotiations for British entry highlighted, the European Community has had and will have profound effects on the outside world: on exporters of temperate foodstuffs like the United States, Australia, and Canada; on producers of tropical products like Latin America and Africa; on the market for light manufactures from developing countries like India and Pakistan; and on the trade patterns of other European nations like Scandinavia, Switzerland, and Austria.

The GATT negotiations will offer a chance to deal constructively with some of these issues. For the advanced nations around the rim of the Community, reciprocal tariff cuts can ease the impact of the common external tariff. By reducing trade barriers jointly, the Atlantic nations can open markets for the less-developed countries more readily than they could do separately. And the trade negotiations could help smooth the way for future British entry into the Community, by anticipating some of the dislocations in trading patterns and facilitating adjustments in advance.

The success of the GATT negotiations will depend on the United States as well as the Community. On some issues the United States will have to adopt a more flexible attitude. In agriculture, for example, undue U.S. pressure could drive the Germans into the arms of the French. And the United States must at least examine closely European suggestions for agreements to provide greater stability for reciprocal tariff concessions, for example, by limiting subsequent escape clause actions and by dealing with significant non-tariff obstacles to trade.

For our purposes, it is fortunately not necessary to treat any of these complex issues in detail. Their relevance for our analysis is to emphasize the point with which this chapter started. The Atlantic partnership is vital for its members, but not only for them. These advanced democratic nations must furnish the core of wider international order. With their economic and political advantages, their policies and actions establish the international framework for much of the rest of the world. Their ability to discharge the obligations implicit in this great power depends on their cooperating intimately within an Atlantic partnership. That is why the partnership is essential not only for the security and welfare of the Atlantic nations themselves, but also as the foundation for a viable order embracing other developed nations like Japan and the older Commonwealth and the less-developed nations of Asia, Africa, and Latin America.

THE FUTURE ORDER

The long-term program to construct an integrated European Community and an Atlantic partnership of equals is a deliberate and creative response to the necessity for shaping a future order. After a decade of progress, this endeavor has reached a critical stage. In the midst of inevitable growing pains, the Community and Atlantic ties are endangered by de Gaulle's challenge to the basic conception. Handling this predicament will test the skill and patience of the United States and the other members of the Community.

The experience of the first decade of the Community provides guidance for the present situation. In 1950, its architects were aware that it might take a long time for Britain to revise its basic attitude toward Europe. Undeterred by that or by the later EDC defeat, they went ahead with practical steps toward their aim. It took ten years of experience to convince British leaders and public that Britain should try to join Europe. It seems clear that no other course would have succeeded in doing so.

The lesson is obvious. In the present situation, the United States and the Europeans should persist in the program to build a strong Europe and a firm Atlantic partnership. That is the right course for its own sake. It also offers the best prospect of confronting de Gaulle with conditions which will show his purposes are not attainable.

No one can say with confidence whether General de Gaulle would then modify his policies as he has done in the past. Once it became clear that the other Five could not be dragged along, then de Gaulle would have to face those facts. An isolated France is not an attractive position for de Gaulle: his aims will be served only if France can speak for Europe and use Europe for its platform.

It is true that de Gaulle could destroy what has been created up to now. But in doing so, he would harm France as much or more than other members of the Community. Strong French interests might well seek to block such self-defeating actions. Few Frenchmen wish to see a return to the national rivalries which wracked Europe in the past. And even if de Gaulle continues to block action, as he may, a clear course by the other Five and the United States will at least have laid the basis for forward motion when de Gaulle no longer governs.

This contest nicely illustrates the interaction of the three major requisites for a foreign policy oriented to shaping a world order. The decisive factor may ultimately be conviction and perseverance. But these take on their meaning and underpinning from the consensus on the long-range goals of European unity and partnership and agreed programs for moving toward them. Together they provide the keys to an effective policy.

3

The Fusion of
Planning and Action

Our discussion thus far has sought to explore and illustrate the components required for a foreign policy which seeks to influence the future in a period of far-reaching change. It has suggested that these requisites are: a strategic framework to integrate interests, objectives, and means; the concerting of mid-range purposes and actions from day-to-day; and steadiness and patience in pursuing them.

Now I want to consider more specifically what these requisites imply in terms of organizing and managing foreign policy.

THE NEED FOR PLANNING

Until recently, relations between states were handled largely by negotiations between ambassadors and foreign ministers. Changing conditions have transformed not only the substance of foreign relations, but the methods for carrying them on. From this point of view, what are the salient features?

Under modern conditions, foreign relations must be envisaged as intensive operations extending into every quarter of the world. In most countries, foreign states and international agencies, with the consent of the host state, are carrying on diverse activities which involve foreign officials in the domestic life of those communities. Under NATO and other alliances, collective defense has meant joint military plans, and foreign forces, bases, supply services, military assistance and training in the allied countries. In most developing countries, besides the usual embassy, the United States, for example, has an AID mission, a U.S. Information Service, and various attachés— agricultural, commercial, military; and it may have a Military Assistance mission (or MAAG). American or other foreign officials may be working with fiscal, economic, and planning agencies of the local government; they may be carrying out exchanges for education and cultural purposes, providing technicians and scientific material of many kinds, furnishing agricultural commodities, and perhaps training and planning with its military as well. All this is in addition to the political contacts and reporting normal to any embassy.

These manifold activities require thousands of decisions and actions at home and abroad. Many are made on the spot by the ambassador, the AID, USIS, or MAAG chief, or by technicians or subordinates. Some must be referred to Washington for decision at various levels in the official hierarchy. The desk officer in the appropriate agency may handle some; others may have to go to an assistant secretary or his equivalent, or to an under secretary, or to the Secretary of State, or to the head of another agency involved. The most basic issues or disputes can be settled only by the President. These far-flung activities, utilizing the most diverse tools—political, economic, military, propaganda, cultural, scientific inevitably engage many different departments and agencies of government, including those whose main duties are in the domestic field. It has been estimated that sixteen or more of such agencies are directly concerned with foreign relations, and another score are less directly involved.

The dependence on joint action is another characteristic of modern foreign affairs. Most of the activities to influence the external environment require working intimately with other nations. In collective defense, in assisting development, in maintaining conditions for prosperity in the developed nations, success depends on cooperation among interested countries. This necessity largely explains the vast expansion of international, regional and *ad hoc* agencies since the war. Their proliferation has greatly complicated the administration of foreign affairs. In the year from July 1, 1961, to June 30, 1962, for example, the United States took part in some 474 international conferences, aside from consultation in continuing bodies like the NATO Council.

As I have stressed, modern foreign affairs must be directed to long-term purposes. Whether one looks at Europe, the less-developed world, or the Soviet bloc, the primary concern must be with shaping the course of events and evolution over an extended period of time. Normally any single action or decision will have only a very limited impact. Our capacity to influence the longer outcome will depend on how far we are able to cumulate our actions and their effects. To accomplish this, the diverse measures must follow a coherent pattern at any one time and over the longer term. They must reinforce one another and be consistent with the larger aim.

In short, foreign relations today consist largely of doing things all over the world; doing them with others; and doing them for long-term results. To be effective, these diverse and far-flung activities must be organized, concerted, and directed.

In terms of managing foreign policy, this means that planning must permeate decisions and action at every level. The purpose of planning in foreign affairs is not primarily to prepare detailed blueprints for handling possible contingencies which might occur in some future period. Its main function is to relate current actions to future consequences and objectives. Its premise is that wise action now must take account of how it may affect the future. In that light it asks: What to do? With whom? By what means? Thus, the integrating of planning and operations is the method by which our requisites for effective policy are achieved in practice.

The selection of long-term objectives and of the priorities necessary to obtain them is one essential form of planning. Such a basic framework must rest on appraisals of the forces at work, including the purposes of other nations, and on judgments as to the measures most likely to influence them favorably. As we have seen, such a strategic framework can provide a sense of direction and general guidelines which can serve to orient more detailed programs and actions.

At a second level, planning is also necessary to coordinate programs of actions such as those relating to one foreign country. Again this does not mean making a blueprint for all future actions. The purpose is more modest —to identify major purposes and targets and establish priorities or scales of relative importance within which day-to-day decisions can be made. Such planning can force us to confront dilemmas such as whether to bolster an existing regime in the hope of achieving at least temporary stability, or whether to accept turmoil and disorders as the price of reform that is essential to lay the basis for social, economic, or political progress. Unplanned action may only squander our limited influence.

Planning must serve a third function, that of equipping ourselves for future needs. Many of the instruments for action or influence require a long time to produce.

The lead time in military items is familiar. Lead times also exist in many other fields. Knowledge of areas undergoing political or economic change cannot be attained overnight. Training people for such special skills or tasks may take years, as the Herter Committee report on "Personnel for the New Diplomacy" stresses; and hence it is essential to anticipate the kinds of skills which may be needed for future actions. But even here the purpose is not to try to predict specific crises which may arise, but rather to allow us to start now to equip ourselves with the skills and instruments for conditions which can be foreseen.

Hence planning is the handmaiden or counterpart of effective action. It creates the framework and basis for organizing and concerting effort and for directing it to suitable ends.

How well are the institutions, traditions, and the practices of the United States suited to carrying on these diverse activities in a coordinated way jointly with others? How can our institutions be used most effectively to achieve our long-range purposes? How can we concert better with others? These questions concern not only ourselves, but also many other parts of the world. Our power and influence are less dominant than fifteen years ago, but they are still immense. And the duty to lead still rests on us, though much more depends now upon our capacity to elicit cooperation.

THE ROLE OF THE SECRETARY OF STATE

Under our system the President has the primary authority and responsibility for handling foreign affairs. In the nuclear age his role has indeed become awesome. As Chief Executive he heads the vast federal bureaucracy at home and overseas. As Commander-in-Chief he controls the armed forces and the nuclear arsenal. Television, radio, and press give him unique access to the public.

In conducting foreign affairs, however, he must have the cooperation of many others. For the instruments of foreign policy, he requires the support of Congress in passing laws, voting appropriations, and approving treaties. For making and executing policy, he must rely on a chain of officials extending from Washington into remote villages overseas. And for effective action, he must obtain the active cooperation of many other nations.

Even so the President is the keystone of the arch. Only he has power to control and direct members of the Cabinet, to arouse public support for essential programs, or to cement relations with allies. Only if the President uses his powers to the full can any important policy obtain the necessary support in the Executive branch, the Congress, and the country.

Many factors tend to push questions and crises to the President's desk for decision. Where issues involve several agencies, only his authority can settle disputes finally. The steady stream of official visitors to Washington bring in their train many questions to the President. The ghastly costs of mistakes induce an attitude of caution and hesitation to delegate.

Yet there is no escape from delegating most of the decisions and actions in foreign affairs. Given the limits on his time and energy, the President could handle only a tiny fraction of the specific decisions, even if he did nothing else. But he cannot afford to become wholly engrossed even in important detailed decisions. His task is also to ensure the integration of policy-making in Washington and the coordination of programs and actions abroad. Yet he cannot do this by himself either. He can and must, however, create the conditions which will enable it to be done on his behalf.

To make this possible, the President, in my opinion, must do two things: he must make the Secretary of State his chief of staff in foreign affairs; and he must establish the basic framework of policy which sets the main guidelines and priorities. Both elements seem indispensable for effective policy-making and execution.

By tradition, the Secretary of State is considered the chief adviser of the President on foreign policy, despite historic exceptions. Under postwar conditions, however, with so many more departments and agencies involved, he must be much more. The Secretary of State must be able to act for the President in weaving the threads of policy into a coherent pattern on a wide range of matters. In the recent past, General Marshall and Mr. Acheson filled this role under President Truman; and so did Mr. Dulles under President Eisenhower.

Among the Cabinet officers, the Secretary of State should be the obvious choice to serve as the President's chief of staff for foreign affairs. The Secretary and his department should have the broadest view and widest competence in this field. With a worldwide network of representatives abroad, the Secretary and his department should be in the best position to draw on the requisite information and breadth of view. Within the department is the largest staff of experts on all parts of the world with actual experience as to local conditions.

Members of the White House staff cannot perform this function for the President. They have an important job to do in seeing that the President is adequately informed, and that problems are brought to his attention. They can serve as his eyes and ears. But no matter how talented, they cannot substitute for the Secretary of State in integrating policy and programs. They lack the necessary staff in Washington and overseas. Their attention will necessarily shift from crisis to crisis and from subject to subject. They cannot possibly provide the constant supervision and steady direction essential for the exercise of continuing influence over an extended period of time. The Secretary and his department must do that.

To integrate the many strands of foreign activities into a coherent whole, however, requires an unusual collection of talents. The Secretary and the department will be able to assert and maintain preeminence in this integrating function only if they have the skills and capacities to perform it. The Secretary himself must have great intellectual capacity and energetic leadership. The department must have a staff which is able, imaginative, and expert. The other departments must accept the leading role of the Department of State, and it must exercise its leadership with restraint. It will be dealing with many departments having experts in their specific fields. If it is to enjoy their respect, it will have to bring to these special fields sufficient competence to understand and handle the basic problems.

But, above all, the President himself must look to the Secretary of State and to the department to fulfill these functions and must at all times provide the necessary backing. If he does so, the Secretary of State can wield the authority of the President to a sufficient degree to see that the activities of the government as a whole are carried out in a coherent and coordinated way. But if the Secretary does not assert his prerogative, or if the President does not support him, then there is no effective way of coordinating the activities of the Executive branch in the making of policy in Washington or in the far-flung operations overseas.

Even with the requisite confidence and talents, however, the President, the Secretary of State, and the department will not be able to perform their respective roles without a reasoned framework of basic policy establishing the basic objectives of policy and a scale of priorities among them. This framework must reflect the President's convictions, must be understood and accepted by all the departments and agencies, and must be adhered to as a guide to decision within the Executive branch. Such a framework can also help identify the kinds of instruments that will be needed for both the present and the future. It can facilitate our relations with other countries by identifying common interests calling for cooperation. It provides the foundation for organized support in Congress and the country.

Within the Executive branch such guidelines are an essential basis for delegating decisions to successive levels of the bureaucracy. The teamwork among departments and agencies and representatives overseas depends on understanding the direction and objectives of our policy. Without this, there is little reason to expect their many actions to form the coherent pattern needed to have an impact on events. Such a strategy cannot of course furnish automatic answers on specific issues. Supporting activities and policies must be based on far more intensive analysis of specific factors. But without such a starting point, concrete issues are likely to be approached and settled in isolation on a pragmatic basis. And unless decisions can be related to broader purposes, the result may be to confuse the Congress and our own public and make it harder to obtain support and cooperation from other nations.

The National Security Council (NSC) was created in 1947 in recognition of the need for a basic national strategy. At that time the primary focus was on integrating foreign, military, and economic policies. Now far more strands must be woven together. The function of the NSC has often been misunderstood. It is not a separate policy-making agency and was not intended to be. It is a forum in which the departments can expose and discuss their views with the President on some of the basic issues of policy. Therefore, it is not a substitute for continuing able staff work in the departments. On the contrary, it depends entirely on their carrying on such staff work and planning as a basis for their participation in the NSC.

In the Eisenhower administration, the NSC was probably overloaded with matters of lesser importance in the effort to cover too many fields of policy through NSC papers. Even so, the NSC did fulfill an essential function in the work of making a basic strategy. The regular discussion among the main Cabinet officers and the President, on the basis of previously circulated papers, was valuable in focusing their attention and that of their staffs on long-range aspects of policy.

The Kennedy administration tended to use the NSC much less. It was sensible, I think, to cut back on the number and scope of subjects covered, and to simplify the paperwork and procedures. But the reaction may have gone too far. In my view, the NSC Planning Board, which brought together assistant secretaries and their counterparts from the key departments and agencies to prepare staff papers for the Council, was useful. To some extent this function is now performed more informally by sessions with the Special Assistant to the President and by task forces or special committees. Of course, many matters have to be handled separately with Cabinet members individually or jointly, but this can hardly take the place of the wider discussion on the basis of prepared papers which have been made available beforehand for staff analysis in the departments.

Whatever the procedure, much of the help in integrating national policy must come from the Department of State. In this, the Policy Planning Staff, now called the Policy Planning Council, has an important role to play. Under its various directors, its approach to planning has been along the lines already discussed—not to prepare paper plans for the remote contingency, but to bring to bear on current actions or problems thinking about longer range aspects or implications. This staff has been small ever since its formation in 1947 under Secretary Marshall. By no means was it expected to carry on all the planning required within the department and it has never undertaken to do this. On the contrary, its special role has always been to take the overall view on foreign policy, and to analyze basic forces and the main lines of policy needed to cope with them. The intention has always been that the regional bureaus should also plan with respect to their areas. This concept, however, has too often not been adequately carried out. In some regional bureaus, planning officers have contributed significantly, but in most, they have had only limited influence on the work of the bureau.

In developing an adequate basic strategy, the integrating of military and political aspects has been especially difficult. In our period, military strategy always has major political overtones or components. The concept of deterrence blends both elements together. Collective defense normally requires the support and cooperation of allies on strategic concepts, the composition of forces, and bases. And the kinds of forces available or planned have a direct bearing on the conduct of foreign policy. The handling of crises may be seriously handicapped if weapons or forces are ill-suited to the need or their use would produce unduly damaging political effects. Again, in the less-developed countries it is essential to relate military assistance programs and force levels to other objectives such as growth and political stability, and this may pose difficult choices as well as negotiation with allies or recipients of such assistance. Finally, arms control clearly involves the interrelation of political and military aspects.

Great strides have been made in relating foreign policy and military policy, but the problem is not yet solved. Undoubtedly, successive Secretaries of State and Defense usually seek to work together. But the budget process, in which many of the decisions are made, does not normally give an effective voice to the Secretary of State or his department. Moreover, it must be said that often the department has not had adequate staff experts to enable the Secretary to play a sufficiently strong role in this field. In consequence his advisory function on military matters frequently has been inadequately fulfilled or gone by default.

If the Secretary of State and his department do not discharge their functions in developing and integrating basic policy, the course of policy-making in Washington is likely to be erratic and *ad hoc*. The lack of proper guidelines will also impede coherent action down the line and dissipate our influence in many situations.

COORDINATION OF PROGRAMS

Even with an adequate framework of basic policy, the Secretary of State and his department have a further task to perform on behalf of the President. This is to coordinate programs of action to carry out agreed policies. The diverse activities of many departments and agencies, in Washington and the field, must be concerted to ensure that they reinforce each other.

In 1953 the need for a better inter-agency coordination was stressed in the Report of the Jackson Committee appointed by President Eisenhower. On the basis of that report, the Operations Coordinating Board (OCB) was created for the purpose of encouraging such coordination and programing. The Under Secretary of State was chairman, and similar officials from other departments were members. The OCB spawned a network of committees staffed mainly by officers from the interested agencies. They doubtless served some useful purposes in causing the various officers to get together for discussion. The process generated masses of planning papers and progress reports. But it would be an exaggeration to say that OCB succeeded in meeting the need for really integrated programs.

In the field, the creation of the "country team" under the ambassador was designed to unify action among the various U.S. agencies. This concept has improved operations materially when the Ambassador has executive capacity and broad interests. But since specialized officers of AID, USIS, or MAAG are still instructed from their own agencies, this highlights the need for coordination in Washington.

In 1961, the Kennedy administration abolished the OCB and placed the responsibility for coordination directly on the Department of State. This method, if backed fully by the President, should probably be more effective for achieving the desired results. One handicap in the OCB was the absence of clear leadership. The change could correct this weakness.

The Herter Committee on Foreign Affairs Personnel in 1962 endorsed the placing of this duty of coordination on the Department of State. But it recognized that the department "has not developed adequately either the attitudes or the machinery needed to relate policies to the operations required to carry them out." This shortcoming has several causes.

One, as the Herter Committee said, is that "the traditional concept of the Foreign Service diplomat has not fostered what might be called a 'programing sense.'"

Another is the competing claims on the assistant secretaries and their immediate associates, who might be expected to do the job of coordination. Current crises compete with the long-run programing for their attention, and ordinarily the short-run demands win out. This is hardly surprising, considering the scope of duties of an assistant secretary. He is expected to oversee the answering of innumerable cables to and from the field. He must appear before congressional committees to testify on the budget, on specific proposals, and for investigations. He must keep the press informed about activities in his area, and answer their inquiries. He must maintain contact with foreign ambassadors in Washington from the countries in his area. And finally, he must administer his bureau and supervise the selection and transfer of personnel in the department and for embassies overseas. Naturally this set of demands is more than the assistant secretary can perform, even with competent help. As a result, he has very little time indeed for programing or coordination.

In his place, the programing for a country might be performed by the desk officer responsible for that country. Unfortunately this is not an adequate solution as things stand. He too has his hands so full with specific duties from day to day that it is hard for him to focus on planning or programing so as to relate the parts to some larger whole. Moreover, in recent years the desk officer has tended to be relatively subordinate in rank. He has less seniority, and often much less experience, than the ambassador or ministers on the embassy staff. With only limited authority and influence, he is not always well equipped to coordinate programs and decisions on his country and to backstop the ambassador.

To improve the capacity of the department to translate policies into programs of action, the Herter Committee proposed a new post of Executive Under Secretary of State. His function would be to integrate policies, programs, and administration.

This might well be a useful step. But the question would still remain as to how he can fulfill these responsibilities. With missions in a hundred countries, the work of programing will have to be done lower down. To make this possible, the country desk officer, or other official in the department, will have to have the responsibility to prepare plans with other interested agencies, but with authority for considerable leadership. Obviously, for most countries it is not feasible to draw detailed blueprints for the next few years. What is possible, however, is to try to appraise the political, economic, and social factors which are relevant to our purposes, and to consider how our instruments can be most effectively used to influence or modify these forces, and by what means.

In performing this task, the country team directed by the ambassador should have a central role. In practice, however, the country team does not appear ordinarily to do much planning or to have an active part as adviser for Washington in this respect. This is most regrettable. The country team, located on the spot, should have the fullest and most intimate knowledge about local conditions and the best feel for what kinds of actions may or may not be effective and suitable. Yet the typical embassy staff does not contain an officer, or officers, charged with the duty to plan and specially qualified to perform it. In order to strengthen the programing within each country, one obvious step would be to add to the embassy staff officials properly equipped for preparing such plans, and to expect the embassy to take the initiative in doing so.

WORKING WITH OTHERS

The discussion thus far has been concerned with the machinery of the United States for making and carrying out foreign policy. Beyond that are the means for working with others which are so distinctive a feature of foreign relations under modern conditions. With interdependence steadily growing, the mechanisms for concerting policies and activities with other nations become steadily more important.

That machinery now takes many forms, regional and world-wide. The United Nations and its specialized agencies constitute a major segment of the framework of international order and cooperation. Any effort to examine the activities and operations of these institutions would open up much too wide a range of issues for proper treatment here. Consequently, I will confine this discussion to a few comments on the concerting of effort among the Atlantic nations.

Much of this is still done bilaterally but major joint activities are multilateral, especially through NATO for collective defense and political coordination, through the Organization for Economic Cooperation and Development (OECD) for economic and monetary policy, and through its Development Advisory Committee for assistance to the less-developed countries. Thus the machinery for concerting policy and action among the Atlantic nations is concerned with relations directly among themselves and with joint policy toward the Soviet bloc and the less-developed countries.

In the previous chapter, I discussed some of the problems in working with our European partners arising from differences in outlook, influence, and obligations. The relations among the Atlantic nations are in transition. With returning self-confidence, the European desire for influence reflecting their combined strength, or at least their potential, creates major strains within the partnership. The European Community cannot yet represent them jointly for most purposes and the disparity in power means that its separate members cannot have the same influence as the United States on the common policy, whatever the forms or fictions.

It seems probable that no real solution can be had unless and until a united Europe emerges which is capable of speaking and acting with one voice. In the meantime, however, some steps could be taken to improve the concerting of effort. In 1957, NATO, on the basis of a report by three "Wise Men," adopted various proposals to strengthen political consultation. Since then the NATO Council has achieved more mutual understanding and coordinated action among the members, and the more active role of the Secretary General has also been helpful. But there is still need to improve coordination among the Atlantic nations on political, economic, and military planning and policy. Divided views on the Congo, Berlin, Laos, or on NATO strategy or measures for arms control are costly to the common interests. They show the urgent need for better processes for agreeing on these interests and on specific actions and tactics for pursuing them. Several steps might be useful.

One fruitful course might be to develop a procedure for bringing key officials from capitals regularly to consult together on specific issues. The foreign policy of each NATO member is made at home by officials responsible for decisions and action. The members of the NATO Permanent Council are not directly in this stream of policy-making. Relying on instructions, they can rarely be fully informed on the details of all the matters considered. Hence on the most crucial issues, the Council is, at best, only a pale substitute for meetings directly among the key officials who will be deciding or advising on these issues.

The OECD has recognized this basic fact about policy-making and adapted its methods to reflect it. Within the OECD framework, key officials from each of the capitals meet together on fiscal, economic, and monetary policy. As policy-makers, they are able to examine jointly the full range of relevant factors more readily than permanent delegates dependent on cables for information and instructions. Back at home, they provide a direct link between national decisions and any consensus reached among the partners. And even if agreement cannot always be reached, the chance to explore frankly the reasons for divergence may prevent differing actions from provoking further cleavages or frictions. This process has succeeded notably in concerting thinking and in producing joint approaches to common problems.

There is no reason why the same methods should not work within the NATO framework. Indeed, this procedure has been used on a small scale among the planning officials of the key countries. It could readily be extended to assistant secretaries and others on a wide range of politics and problems.

A second step should be to improve the machinery for NATO military planning and especially for integrating the military and political factors. In part, the frictions and tensions on strategic and other issues can be traced to the absence of an adequate mechanism for handling them. The Standing Group and Military Committee of NATO have not met this need. SACEUR, the Supreme Commander at SHAPE, has partially filled this vacuum by providing a channel for the views of European allies. But this tends to distort his role in the alliance.

It would be much better to create a civilian post in NATO corresponding to a defense minister for the alliance. With a qualified staff of civilian and military experts, he could assist in achieving consensus on alliance-wide strategy and force goals and in working with members on their military programs and plans.

Third, the idea of a small steering committee for NATO should be candidly examined. On it would be the major members (Britain, Federal Republic, France, Italy, and the United States), the Secretary General, with perhaps a rotating member to represent the smaller countries.

Such a group would partly meet the pressure for a larger European voice in alliance affairs. The experience with the restricted Berlin working party indicates that this could offer an effective and practical way to confront problems in common. In the past, such proposals have been opposed by the smaller members. Actually the crucial issues seldom turn on divergences between large and small, and the interests and views of the smaller members could in any case be reflected through the rotating member and the Secretary General. If such a group can improve the cohesion of the alliance, the smaller members will share the benefits.

A fourth innovation might be tried in order to promote consensus on basic objectives. While the European Community is still developing, frictions among the Atlantic nations may cause parochial concerns to obscure the basic interests and tasks they have in common.

The experience of the European Community may suggest a useful method for mitigating this problem. The impartial Commissions of the Community have shown the value of having a group which does not speak for member governments, but attempts to look at issues from the overall or general viewpoint. This same function could be performed for the Atlantic nations by four or five respected individuals of international standing who did not exercise any delegated authority. They would be chosen for their independence and should speak only for themselves.

Their task would be to analyze the overall position of the Atlantic nations in relation to the wider world situation and especially to identify more precisely their common interests and to propose policies to promote them. Their reports could be put before the NATO Council of Ministers at their regular meetings. They would have only the status which the standing of their members might command. They would, however, be on the agenda for discussion as a matter of course.

At first sight such an arrangement might appear to be so fragile as to be useless. Yet one of the difficulties in the Atlantic alliance has been that national interests too often take precedence over the more basic joint interests of its members. The effect is to downgrade, or disregard, the common interests. If the suggested procedure focused attention on joint interests and policies, it might have the benefit of raising discussions to a higher level. This has been the result within the European Community, and it has probably been as valuable as the formal authority of the Commission.

These measures would not be a panacea or a final structure for Atlantic partnership. They might, however, help the Atlantic nations in concerting policy and actions among themselves, especially in the awkward period while relations between the United States and the European Community are evolving.

Within the wider non-Communist world, the major task of the Atlantic nations is assisting the less-developed countries to modernize. In this field, the large number of assisting nations and agencies presents two problems in concerting effort. If not coordinated, the various forms of assistance may distort development or dissipate and waste scarce local resources in unwise ventures. And the multiple sources of aid may erode its influence in fostering wise choices by the recipient country.

To some extent these dangers can be mitigated if the recipient country has a strong planning agency and a coherent program for development. Indeed that seems an indispensable foundation for effective cooperation. Hence the Western nations should encourage and assist the formation and operation of such planning and programing agencies, through the International Bank, the UN Special Fund, the OECD Development Center, and private institutions.

The granting of assistance can also be coordinated in two ways. In providing bilateral aid, the various countries can act jointly through consortia, organized by the International Bank, or by the Development Advisory Committee of OECD, or perhaps in other ways. These can insure that the outside help reinforces a development program scrutinized on behalf of the group. In addition, the Atlantic nations could well channel more assistance through international agencies like the International Bank, the International Development Agency, the UN Special Fund, and the Inter-American Bank. Such agencies have two advantages over bilateral aid. Since a recipient nation may be less suspicious of political motives, it may be less hesitant about accepting advice from such an agency. And for similar reasons, the agency itself can be stricter in applying criteria of self-help without the charge of undue interference.

STAYING POWER

In managing foreign policy in our time, the most troublesome question of all is how to achieve the staying power required for the long-term challenge facing us. The tasks—building Europe and an Atlantic partnership, modernizing the less-developed countries, and containing the Soviet Union and China—will all take several decades of steady and demanding effort.

Continuity and persistence are keys to influencing the outcome. They are requisites to make our resources and actions achieve a cumulative effect over time. They are also vital to our capacity to work with other nations for common ends. Their readiness and ability to align their policies and actions with ours will depend largely on sharing a sense of direction and steadfastness in pursuing it. And conversely these qualities will determine the impact of our policies and action on Soviet and Chinese purposes and priorities. They will be induced to modify their aims or their concepts only if convinced of the tenacity of the United States and its allies in resolutely blocking their expansionism. Thus the capacity for persistence in pursuing long-term purposes is a crucial factor in the actual power to shape the future.

The effort to do so will severely test our institutions and our maturity as a nation. The measures needed will be costly and demanding. The progress in each major field will inevitably be slow and halting, and hard to demonstrate. The route is bound to be marked by disheartening failures and tensions. As the United States and a growing European Community try to find their proper relation, both sides will often feel frustrated and resentful. Many of the underdeveloped countries will surely undergo severe political and social upheavals and turmoil through long periods, with halting economic and social progress, often offset by growth of population. No one can be sure how the internal evolution of Soviet society will affect the control of the Communist Party or its policies for outward expansion. Even if the Soviet Union tends to mellow, the process is likely to be fitful with many ups and downs. Communist China allows no ground for even such optimism in the near future. If the tension between China and the Soviet Union continues unabated, it is hard to foresee what the effects may be on Soviet policy or on Communist Chinese actions. And if the Soviets should become less aggressive, many in the West will be unduly eager to drop our guard prematurely. Thus, excessive despair or optimism could cause a slackening of support for the essential policies.

In many ways, our institutions are not well-adapted

to long-term enterprises. In Congress, an annual budget cycle and the bi-annual elections tend to focus on the short-run results of any policy or action. Yet one or two years are much too short a period in which to measure progress on most of these fronts. They are not too short, however, to reveal specific shortcomings or failures. Since these are certain to occur and may be serious, congressional and electoral attention will highlight the failures and defects rather than the longer-term benefits or improvements.

The same tendency is even more marked in the press. Its coverage is by nature predisposed against adequate reporting of such long-term policies. The mistakes will all be covered in detail as headline news. Gradual progress toward partnership with Europe, or toward growth in the less-developed countries, or toward the achieving of our policies toward the Communist bloc, is much less likely to be newsworthy. The reason is not prejudice on the part of the press, but simply a professional outlook as to what is news.

Our traditions and attitudes also are not conducive to a policy of the sort required. In general our national bent is to demand prompt solutions for problems. Our domestic experience has created an undue confidence in our capacity to deal with issues and an impatience with delays. Any situation which has to be lived with or which progresses only slowly is likely to cause frustration or resentment. Moreover, our pragmatic, or engineering, approach tends to tackle issues one at a time, or separately. Creating a broad framework or strategy and relating specific actions or decisions to it does not come naturally. Such a framework seems an artificial constraint.

Impatience also generates undue pressure for novelty. When a course of action does not produce rapid results, there are likely to be demands to reverse or change it. Sticking with a long-term program until it has had time to work often gives rise to charges of rigidity or lack of imagination. Finally the faith in compromise to resolve any dispute can be a source of weakness. A proper policy toward de Gaulle, for example, will seem to many to be too inflexible. In the same way, many still find it impossible to believe that the struggle with the Soviet Union and China could not be promptly "settled" with mutual concessions.

The annual battle over foreign aid illustrates our problem. Each year the case for assistance must be made anew, without really being able to show specific results from the very large expenditures. Opponents can parade instances of mistakes, or mishandling, or worse. With luck some situations can be shown to have improved at least slightly; others can hardly be displayed with satisfaction.

These various tendencies create severe handicaps to

long-term policy. To surmount them is not easy. Yet in retrospect the United States has performed reasonably well in the postwar world. The record is far from perfect; there have been mistakes and delays. But despite the novelty and magnitude of the problems, the country did reorient its policies, assume the leadership inherent in its power, and devote vast resources to defense, assistance and related purposes.

The key to this result has been political leadership, especially by the President. Earlier we discussed his essential role in organizing and concerting policy and execution within the government. At least as important is his role as leader of public opinion. Others, like Cabinet members or a Senator Vandenberg, can contribute materially. But they cannot substitute for the President in developing public understanding of our situation and what it demands. Quite clearly it is not feasible to make every man his own Secretary of State. No citizen concerned with his family, his business, his local community, his church, can possibly devote enough time to foreign affairs to master many of the specific issues. But that is not necessary. Public opinion in foreign affairs is formed by only a fraction of the electorate. And such citizens can understand the broad lines of policy and the reasons for them if they are adequately explained. They are quite capable of grasping ideas about the basic forces at work in the world, the role of the United States and its interests, and the general courses of action which are necessary in order to cope with such problems.

Moreover, if properly explained, these matters can be seen as a challenge, not merely as burdens. The success of the Peace Corps shows that this notion is not merely imaginary. In our time, the outside world offers an arena for applying our talents and stretching our horizons as did the opening of our West more than a century ago. The chance to play a creative part in shaping a future order should be viewed as a similar challenge.

In essence, the forces remolding the world reflect the triumph of ideals for which our civilization has stood for many generations. The notion that men should govern themselves and work out their own destiny has been the energizing idea of the new nations in their struggle for independence. Just as happened in Europe, many of the nations will doubtless endure autocratic or oligarchic regimes before achieving government by consent, but the demands for dignity and self-respect will sooner or later make themselves effective. The growing ferment within the Soviet Union is the best testimony of the universal appeal of these ideas.

The other great idea which is at work in the world is also of Western origin. This, springing from the industrial revolution, is the notion that man can improve the human lot by effort. For most of the peoples of the globe, this is an explosive new attitude which is bound to generate tremendous pressures to realize it.

It would be a sad thing if Europe and the United States, where these two basic ideas had their origins, were to fail to identify themselves with their full flowering on a global scale. To do so would be to stultify our own best ideals. It would also deprive us and our children of the chance to find meaning for our lives and for theirs in the decades that lie ahead.

Index

NATO, and nuclear issue, 66-74 *passim*

Peace Corps, 111

Planning, 27, 79-84, 105-6; NATO, 65-74 *passim*, 101-2; *see also* Programs

Policy, 10-12; and aid programs, 18-24; de Gaulle's, 51-59; European integration, and the U.K., 40-47; future European Community, 77-78; impact of, and time, 24-27; integration of, 86-93; NATO, 51 (*see also* North Atlantic Treaty Organization); necessity for long-term, 106-10; need for planning, 79-84; nuclear, 65-74 *passim*; periods of divergence, 34; policy-making and working with others, 98-106; and structure of Atlantic alliance, 37-40; today's, 28-35, 78, 106-10; U.S. system of planning, 85-93

Policy Planning Council, 91-92

Politics, 8, 10-11, 45-47 *passim*; and European integration, 13-14, 37-38, 54, 55, 64-65; and less-developed countries, 19, 21-23 *passim*; and long-run aims, 33; and the military, 92-93; and NATO, 99, 100, 101-2; and nuclear issue, 66, 67, 70-72 *passim*; and programming, 27, 94-98 *passim*

President, of the U.S., 85-93 *passim*, 110

Press, 33, 46, 85, 105

Priorities, 28-30, 89

Programs, assistance, 18-24, 104-6; agreed, importance of, 35, 78; coordination of, 94-98; foreign-affairs, 95-98; intermediate, for long-term goals, 27-35 *passim*; necessity of long-term, 106-10; *see also* Planning

Propaganda, 8, 10-11

Public opinion, 33, 46, 85, 90, 108-11 *passim*; *see also* Press

Reform, and aid, 21, 22

Russia, *see* Union of Soviet Socialist Republics

Schroeder, Gerhard, 57

Schuman, Robert, 14-15

Security, 2, 12; and aid, 19-22 *passim*, and Atlantic cooperation, 36, 38, 76; and nuclear policy, 55, 66-74 *passim*

Social conditions, and modernization, 19-23 *passim*

Stability, of less-developed countries, 2, 7, 19, 23

State, Department of, 87-89, 91-93 *passim*

State, Secretary of, role of, 86-98 *passim*; *see also* Cabinet, U.S.

Strategy: basic national military, 90-93; and NATO, 31-32, 34, 48-51; value of an agreed, 29-30, 35

Subversion, Communist, 7-8, 10-11, 26

Supreme Allied Command, Europe (SACEUR), 102

Supreme Headquarters, Allied Powers, Europe (SHAPE), 53, 65, 102

Tariffs, 63-65, 74-76

Technical aid, 18; *see also* Assistance

Threats, as policy instrument, 10-11; *see also* Nuclear weapons

Time, factor of, *see* Continuity

Trade: barriers, lowering of, 74-76; and European cooperation, 17, 37, 57-58, 74-75; Monnet on, 39; negotiations, 27, 63-65; as policy instrument, 10-11